The Giant Book
of Sneaky Feats

The Giant Book of Sneaky Feats

by Tom Ferrell
and
Lee Eisenberg

CASTLE BOOKS

CONTENTS

PART TWO: HIGH, WIDE AND HANDY

PART THREE: ARTS AND CRAFTY

PART FOUR : SO YOU WANT TO BE A STUNTMAN

PART FIVE: TRICKS FOR ALL TRADES

PART SIX: CHEAP THRILLS WITH REAL MONEY

PART SEVEN: KNOT SO FAST, BUSTER!

PART EIGHT: THE POWER TO CLOUD MEN'S MINDS

PART NINE: LOOKY WHAT YOU MADE!

Sneaky Feats

TO OUR MOTHERS

This book is not their fault

INTRODUCTION

Shortly after the creation of man, Cain and Abel, the first two boys on their block, were sitting around with a deck of cards playing War. Cain, for some reason nobody understands, was winning. Abel, who wasn't too swift, but a lot swifter than Cain, suddenly said, "Watch this!" He picked up the deck and cut it a couple of times, using one hand only. Cain tried to appear disinterested. But then Abel placed the deck on his arm and fanned the cards from his elbow to the tips of his fingers. Then, with a mere flick of the hand, Abel flipped the cards over, domino-style.

Cain shifted in his chair as his heart quickened. His reaction was not lost upon Abel. Abel offered the deck to Cain and said in a tone that today, six thousand years later, would be called *condescending*, "Here. Pick a card. Any card. Don't tell me what it is."

Leaping to his feet, Cain snatched the deck and threw it on the ground. "I hate you!" he cried out. "I hate you for your smugness, your cool superior manner. But most of all I hate you for your skill and for what, six thousand years from now, will be known as *condescension*. You know what you are? You're a show-off!"

Abel sensed that Cain's last taunt was intended to wound him deeply. But why should it? Abel had not only proved his superiority over his brother, he'd found glory in the sight of his Maker, and, most important, in his own. Abel, as is well known, grew up to ace out Cain again and again. Finally, years later, Cain got so fed up he slew Abel in an effort to even the score.

And that, gentle reader, is the story of Abel, the very first show-off, and Cain, the very first chump. Note that from the beginning all the elements of the show-off were fully developed in Abel, to wit:

3

Competitiveness. The show-off employs certain skills, either innate or acquired, to defeat, humiliate, impress, or simply amuse somebody else, whether a friend, an enemy or a mere stranger. He who shows off, even in a friendly way, is saying, in effect, to the onlooker: "I can do something you can't do. I am better than you." This explains why Cain grew furious at Abel, so much so that he eventually knocked him off. Cain suffered because he couldn't understand how Abel performed his feats. Cain's anguish of soul was only increased by his consciousness that he didn't know any smart (or dumb) tricks. Consequently, Cain got sore. On the other hand, Abel's Creator rejoiced to see Abel's cleverness, hence the familiar saying "The Lord favors the biggest show-off." And that is as true today as it ever was.

Resourcefulness. More often than not, the show-off is one who realizes, consciously or otherwise, that he has little hope of competing (see above) successfully if he confines his operations to conventional tactics. For an example, observe the recent career of Bobby Riggs. A splendid tennis player in his own day, Riggs came eventually to realize that middle age made it impossible for him to compete against today's best male players. So he decided to play Margaret Court, a woman. Before the match, Riggs showed off by swallowing vast numbers of vitamin pills—and by numerous exhibitions of braggadocio. His antics made his opponent, who probably could have beaten him in a fair match, so nervous that she lost. Later on, Riggs *lost* a match to another woman—an event whose significance we shall explain, but in a paragraph to come. Nevertheless, by playing women rather than men, a tactic many would instantly reject as contemptible, Riggs found instant notoriety (and money). He continues to capitalize, playing regular exhibitions, most of which are marked by one show-off device or another: he'll wear a woman's dress; he'll play while wearing galoshes: he'll take to the side of the court with a number of chairs scattered about.

If Riggs were not a show-off, no young American would ever have heard of him. See?

Thirst for glory. Attention is nice, but for a show-off it's not enough. A man who slips on a banana gets *attention* (and laughter), even more so if he breaks his leg. What the show-off is after, above and beyond attention, is *glory*. Someone who shows off is saying to the onlooker, by implication if not out loud, "I have been blessed with wit, imagination, brilliance, or simply an unusual degree of manual dexterity. These things combined, or any one of them, *make me special*." For a macroscopic example, consider the United States of America. Our country is the mightiest show-off in the world, as its historical mythology reflects: George Washington throwing a dollar across the Rappahannock; Daniel Boone leaving notes around whenever he had kilt a b'ar; Babe Ruth pointing to the place where he intended to hit a home run. The space program of the 1960s was showing off in its purest and most glorious form. To put a man on the moon is to say to the rest of the world: "Look at this! We bet we can put a man on a rocket, shoot him through the black reaches of space, and have him land on his feet on another planet. Ready? Now watch!" And it worked, too. But it might *not* have worked, which brings us to another aspect of the show-off's character....

Courage. The show-off must be competitive and resourceful; when his showing-off succeeds he is consequently glorious as well. But what if he fails? Suppose Washington had thrown the dollar into the soup? Suppose the b'ar had kilt Daniel Boone? Suppose Babe Ruth had popped to the catcher? Showing off is inherently risky. When, for example, the show-off tries to flip a frying egg with one hand and winds up with the egg all over his face, he is laughed at, scorned, put to shame; his bones are licked clean by the onlooking vultures.

If this, of course, were a *perfect* world, people would be more gracious when a show-off embarrassed himself.

5

They would say something like: "Nice form, though, that's for sure. Come on, chin up, try it again. You're tired today, or your wrist hurts, or maybe there was something wrong with the egg." But that's not the world we live in, as the show-off (and everyone else) knows. The world is more like this: "Good! It serves you right! Where does some insecure little twit like you get off trying to impress *me*?! You've made a colossal fool of yourself and I'm glad! Drop dead!" And therefore the show-off, eternally aware of the risk and the consequence of failure, must at all times be courageous. Nothing takes more courage than losing a game nobody asked you to play. And even if you win, there's always the chance you will have beaten some sore loser—like Cain.

Whoever desires the career of a show-off, desires an excellent career, all of the above notwithstanding. But let's face it: *Glory never comes easy*. You win some, you lose some. Fly too close to the sun, or the moon, and you may get burned. Deep in every show-off's heart is this awful knowledge. Holding the pan with the half-fried egg, preparing to flip it one-handed into space, the show-off says to himself: "Here goes. If it works, I'm golden. If it doesn't, I'm cooked. *But it must be done! It's my only chance! Lord, open Thy gates to me!*" The show-off can never forget, no matter how he tries, that for every Charles Lindbergh there's an Amelia Earhart; for every Neil Armstrong there's an Evel Knievel; for every Bobby Riggs who plays Margaret Court, there's a Bobby Riggs who plays Billie Jean King. Yes, the show-off knows all this; and, knowing it, takes a firmer grip on the skillet and launches his puny egg into the infinite, toward the great adventure that is Showing Off.

But we digress. What will you learn from this book and why should you learn it? At the very least—assuming you are not totally illiterate or some kind of perfect gentleman—you will learn how to perform several dozen feats of the mind and body. They will come in handy the next time a party reaches the boring stage, i.e. when nobody is listening to what you are saying. We might as well admit it: it's a lot easier to roll a coin across your knuckles than to actually *think* of something terrific to *say*. And they will come in handy the next time somebody is mentally or physically punishing you. Though showing-off does not assure victory, it usually causes an opponent to lay off for a while. Few are versatile enough to punish and gape at the same time. (But when the novelty wears off, watch out!)

Sneaky Feats will also teach you a *way of life*, the Way of the Show-off. It will make you a more confident person, and a more interesting one. It will enable you to convince others that you really *exist*. It will encourage them to remember you, perhaps forever.

The book, you will see, is divided into four parts. "Playing With Your Food" gives you plenty to do when you're at, near, or under a table. "High, Wide and Handy" provides suggestions for everyone with two hands, even if they're both left ones. "Arts and Crafty" features a number of simple items you can make—and to make others fear and respect you. And "So You Want To Be A Stuntman" gives you an assortment of feats to be used wherever and whenever your wicked little heart desires.

—Tom Ferrell
Lee Eisenberg
January 1, 1975
New York City

7

Part One:
Playing With Your Food

THE ONE-ARMED FRIED EGG

Though it sometimes hurts to admit it, most of a show-off's life is spent eating, sleeping and working, just like ordinary people. We haven't heard of a show-off way to sleep yet, but the subject of eating is endlessly adaptable to those little embroideries and graces that do so much to make life superior. In this respect, the top of the heap is occupied by the world's great chefs, who have spent lifetimes learning how to ignite flaming swords and the like. But one must start somewhere, and a good place to begin is with the fried egg over easy, using one hand only.

But first, a warning. Do not try to learn one-handed egg-flipping unless you already know how to fry an egg over easy in the orthodox two-handed way. Hot fat and frying pans are not to be trifled with by beginners. But let's assume you can already fry an egg safely and satisfactorily, and go on from there to the show-off's way.

Be sure you have the right kind of frying pan, about seven inches in diameter and light enough—aluminum is best—to handle gracefully with one hand. The pan should have high sides. The best, perhaps, is one of those French models whose sides rise in a gradual curve, but any kind will work as long as the sides are not too low.

Heat some fat in the pan. It's *very important*, now, to use as little fat as you can, because you do *not* want to be splashed with hot fat when you reach the flipping stage. The modern non-stick Teflon-surfaced frying pan allows you to use the least fat. When the fat has reached frying heat, you are ready to proceed with the first fancy step as follows:

Break the egg with one hand only. To do this, grasp the egg as shown in figure 1 and give it a determined, but not violent, crack on the side of the pan or any other hard surface. The idea is to produce a fracture running all the way around the egg, without penetrating the yolk. Very swiftly open the egg as shown in figure 2, letting the gooey inside of the egg drop into the pan. It may help you through this step to handle the egg as though it had a hinge at the top between the two halves of the shell. Sometimes, no matter how deft you are, this step fails and all you get is a handful of mess, but that's part of the risk the show-off takes. When it happens, try again with another egg.

Now that the egg is in the pan, just let it sit there a while until one side is done. When only the top of the egg is still wet and uncoagulated, jiggle the pan a bit to make sure the whole thing is free and slides around, instead of sticking to the bottom. Pick up the pan, tilt it slightly away from you, and jiggle the pan until the egg slides downhill and begins to slide up the far side of the pan, as in figure 3. Continue to jiggle and slide until the egg reaches the critical stage (figure 4).

Then, with a short, snappy upward twitch of the pan, persuade the egg to follow the path shown by the arrow in figure 4, until it assumes the position shown in figure 5. Cook the other side until done, and there you have it.

The hardest part about the whole procedure is doing everything quickly but gently enough to avoid breaking the yolk during the flip, when the egg is in the half-cooked stage. One way to learn the procedure without risk is to fry an egg on both sides in the ordinary way, then use the pre-fried egg to practice figures 3 through 5 until you can perform the flip with a minimum of risk and violence. Then invite your friends in for breakfast, put one hand in your pocket, and astonish the world's morning.

SLICING A BANANA WITHOUT PEELING IT

Even the humble banana is useful for showing off. Suppose you give your best friend a banana. He will be surprised, no doubt, but only mildly so. However, imagine his astonishment when he peels the banana and finds that, within the apparently unbroken skin, the banana is already sliced! Before his eyes the whole thing will fall into neat segments as he peels it.

To peel a banana inside its skin, follow these steps:

1) Take a fully-ripe banana and a fine needle, long enough to reach from one side of the banana to the other, threaded with about two feet of fine silk or synthetic thread. Do not use a young, fresh, waxy-looking all-yellow unblemished banana, for it is actually necessary to pierce the skin many times, and you don't want the holes to show. The dull and partially blackened skin of a ripe banana helps conceal the holes.

2) Pierce the banana anywhere along its length, inserting the needle at one of the banana's corners (a banana is not cylindrical, but more like a five-sided prism). Pass the needle under the skin of the banana to the next corner.

15

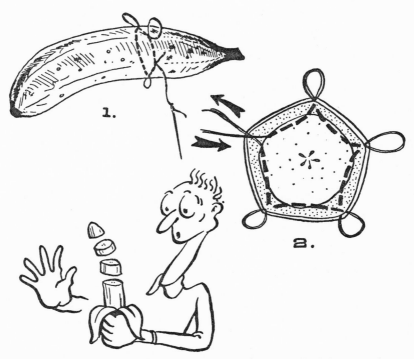

1.

2.

Draw the needle and most of the thread out, but be sure to leave the end of the thread protruding from the original entry point.

3) Insert the needle back into the hole just made in the second corner, and proceed to draw it out through the third corner, and so on until the needle and thread emerge from the original point of entry. A cross-section of the banana at the working site now looks like the drawing.

4) Take both ends of the thread and pull. As the thread is withdrawn through the original entry hole, the flesh of the banana will be sliced through.

Repeat the entire process at different sites along the banana until you have made as many slices as you wish. The banana is now sliced inside its skin. The holes will not be noticeable except on very close inspection. And who is going to look that closely at a banana?

THE SEVEN-LAYER POUSSE-CAFE (HOO-HAH!)

The next time you have important guests over to the house, be a big shot after dinner by making a seven-layer pousse-cafe. Start showing off by pronouncing it right (pooskafay) and explaining that it means coffee-pusher in French. To make it, take seven after-dinner liqueurs of contrasting colors and different specific gravities (specific gravity, which depends on the proportions of water, sugar and alcohol in the beverages, may be determined with a hydrometer from a dealer in laboratory supplies; or a wine-maker's saccharometer will do the job).

Line up the bottles with the heaviest liqueur first and the lightest, which is usually cognac, at the end. For this example we choose: (1) white anisette; (2) creme de cacao; (3) white creme de menthe; (4) apricot liqueur; (5) triple sec; (6) Chartreuse; (7) cognac.

Now, pour a quantity of the heaviest liqueur—in this case, the white anisette—into a spoon and dribble it down the side of a tall, thin liqueur glass. Actually, since this is the bottom layer, it is OK to just slop it in.

Take a like quantity of liqueur number two, the sec-

1.

2.

ond heaviest, and dribble it slowly from the spoon down the side of the glass, so that it does not mix with the liqueur below but floats on it, spreading out into a layer of contrasting color (figure 1).

Repeat the process, being careful not to disturb the glass, until all seven liqueurs are neatly arranged in layers (figure 2). There you have it.

There's more than one way to show off when you drink your seven-layer pousse-cafe. You may sip the product from top to bottom; or, using a long, fine straw, from bottom to top.

Or, instead of making it at home, you may order one in a bar. If the bartender doesn't know how to make it, insist on demonstrating to him. Then, when the whole thing is made with all the layers perfectly arranged after a lot of time and trouble and irritation, just knock the whole thing back in one great gulp!

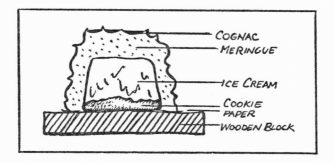

COGNAC
MERINGUE
ICE CREAM
COOKIE PAPER
WOODEN BLOCK

VOILA!
FLAMING BAKED ALASKA!

Showing off at the dinner table begins early in life—with throwing peas, or eating them from a knife. Advanced showing off, however, requires time, preparation, thought, and the sincere desire to astonish. One way is to present guests or members of the family with something to eat that's a real gasper—an irresistible center of attraction and admiration.

Such an object is the Flaming Baked Alaska, or *omelette norvegienne,* which has a wholly exaggerated reputation for difficulty. You, of course, can profit by the reputation; it's best not to make this where people can find out how easy it really is. The following recipe gives you a small product, just right for two people; for a bigger one, use a slice of sponge cake, or a sheet of sugar-cookie dough baked in a slab, for a base, and increase other proportions accordingly.

1. Separate the eggs, dropping the whites in the Mixmaster bowl. If you are unable to keep other people out of the kitchen, impress them now by swallowing the yolks whole; otherwise, throw them away. Add about a third of

a cup of sugar and a pinch of cream of tartar to the egg whites. Then beat like crazy until the meringue is stiff enough that it stands up in little peaks when you withdraw the mixer blades.

2. Take a round half-pint carton of ice cream (peach or strawberry is nice) and a big, thick, hard cookie—Chinese almond cookies are good—about the same size as the big end of the ice-cream carton. The ice cream should be firm but not rock-hard.

Cut a piece of brown paper about an inch bigger than the cookie. Put the paper on a wooden cutting board or similar slab—do not use a metal pan. Put the cookie in the middle of the paper, get the ice cream out of the carton in one piece and put it on the cookie. Slather the meringue all over, sealing carefully—but hurry.

3. Slide the whole thing into the oven, which you have carefully preheated to 500 degrees. Inspect after about two minutes, then keep checking at one-minute intervals. When the meringue is brown in patches on the outside, it's

done. This won't take more than five minutes altogether, so don't forget to keep an eye on it.

4. Pick up the Baked Alaska with a pancake turner and slide it onto a plate, getting rid of the paper if you can. Now, take about an ounce of cognac or a fruit-flavored liqueur such as curaçao, which you have carefully warmed by putting it in a small glass, covering the glass with aluminum foil, and standing it for a few minutes in a pan of hot water (you must warm it because it will not ignite at room temperature). Pour it into the smallest saucepan you have (but one with a long handle) and touch a match to it. (WHOOSH!) Pour it instantly over the Baked Alaska. (SIZZLE!) Be sure the dish you put the Baked Alaska on is big enough so that none of the flaming liqueur will run over the sides onto the table. Present it immediately, before the fire goes out. Make a wish and fall to.

HOW TO CLEAN A FISH

What do we like to do to relax after hours of wowing friends and strangers with mind-boggling tricks? We like to go down to the lake and fish. It isn't actually hard to catch fish—beginners are often as successful as old-timers—so this feat won't provide any flashy tips on angling. Rather, it will help you in the après-catch department, that is, how to clean a fish after you've caught him.

You'll be glad for these tips when you and your partners are standing around muttering, "Yech! Now who is going to touch those icky things and turn them into a tasty meal?" Here's how you can step forward and take control on the spot:

Wash your fish in cold water. Make sure your fish is dead, then place him on the ground. If your fish has fins, cut them off before scaling. A fin can give you an annoying nick. If the fish has scales, take a knife or fish-scaler (there's a dandy from Sweden that sells for around four bucks) and, holding the fish at the tail, scrape carefully forward toward the head (figure 1). You can easily see the scales come off; run your thumb along the fish to feel for any that remain.

Now comes the disgusting part. Like everyone else, fish have gicky stuff inside them. Your job is to get it all out. Using a sharp knife, make a slit up the bottom of the fish, beginning just above the tail and ending right below the head (figure 2). You want to remove the entrails. Once the fish is slit, you'll see them, honest. They come out easily—simply take your knife or hand and flip them out. Make sure to get all of it (gulp).

Chances are, if you're cleaning fish for the first time, you won't want to keep looking at the head anymore. No problem! Take you knife and, your eye and stomach as steady as a brain surgeon's, remove it. It doesn't hurt the fish at all, and it will only make you queasy for a few minutes. Now do the same to the tail, which is a lot easier. Here now is your fish ready for frying or broiling (figure 3). It looks totally innocent, doesn't it?

Please be very careful when cleaning fish. Use a sharp knife and always hold the fish firmly. The worst thing in the world is for a show-off to wear a band-aid. It's humiliating, to say the least.

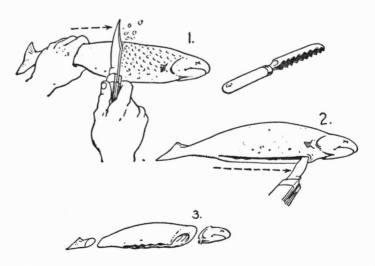

THE CHOPSTICK SCHTICK

There is nothing more inscrutable than eating Chinese food with a fork. It's ridiculously easy to eat with chopsticks—hundreds of millions of people do it every day. Most round-eyed Americans know how to do it, too, but every once in a while you run across a poor chap like the one shown here.

Everyone at the table is throwing down chow mein effortlessly; this fellow, though, picks away at the slippery fare, rice falling on his trousers, lain-drops falling from his head. But as unfortunate as this situation is, imagine his chagrin when he sees you manipulate the mysterious sticks with the wisdom of Confucius. Here's how in two easy steps:

Your first obligation is to establish a stationary stick. Hold it in the crotch of your thumb, as in figure 1, and with the ring finger of that hand. Balance the stick at the most comfortable point.

Your second obligation is to establish a movable stick, as in figure two. Use the tip of your thumb and the second and third fingers. Now make like Groucho Marx (but don't

move your eyebrows, the Chinese didn't find him funny). Pick up your delicious food with the ends of the sticks and shovel it into your mouth. You don't need us to tell you how to do that. Or do you?

A GREAT BALANCING ACT

Among other things, the show-off is a person who knows how to get along when the going gets boring. Say you're at a dinner party and you and the others have told every terrifically funny story you know. The dessert is an upside-down flop, the coffee tastes like sludge, and everyone would rather be home eating crackers in bed.

There are a number of ways to save such an evening and here we'll show you yet another one. All you need are four glasses filled two-thirds with water, as well as three ordinary table knives. The mission: to interlock the knives on three glasses so that the whole construction can hold a fourth glass.

Dare the guests to effect this, telling them they must arrange the knives in triangular fashion, handles on each glass, blades touching at the center.

There are really only a few things you need to know to achieve what this sneaky guy in the drawing is achieving. It comes down to how you interlock the knives. The insert shows all: Knife 1 goes over 2 and under 3. Knife 2 goes over 3 and under 1. Knife 3 goes over 1 and under 2.

This interlocking system should be placed upon the glasses on the sides of the rims facing the center of the construction. Do not balance the knives on both sides of the rim of the glass; this makes the feat look easy. If you do all this correctly, the fourth glass will stand triumphantly on the knives.

THE ALL-WET, INSULTING TIP

The revenge of a show-off can be terrible. Suppose you have stopped off at some roadside hash-house for a cup of coffee and a piece of pie, and you've been disappointed with the pie, the coffee, and the service, not to mention the greasy smells and high prices. How do you get even? By leaving a nickel tip underneath an inverted glass of water is how. This easily-accomplished stunt takes advantage of the well-known fact that atmospheric pressure at sea level is something like fifteen pounds per square inch (less in Colorado, but still enough to work) and therefore will support a column of water.

To do it, take a very full glass of water (if your glass isn't full enough, borrow another and fill yours right up to the brim). Drop the nickel in (see figure 1). Then take a fairly stiff piece of paper of a convenient size and put it over the mouth of the glass.

Now, holding the paper lightly but firmly in place, invert the glass (figure 2). When the glass is upside down remove your hand. The paper—and the water above it, and the nickel—will stay in place. But don't dawdle, because

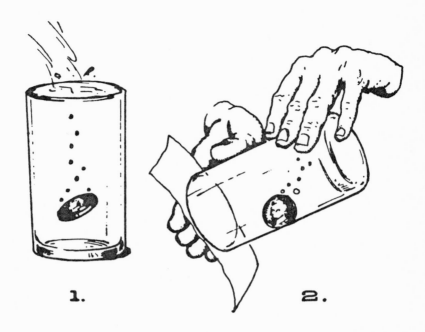

the paper will soak through pretty soon and the whole thing will fall apart.

Set the inverted glass on the counter or table. The top of the counter or table must be Formica or some similar smooth surface; this won't work on a tablecloth, which is why we're teaching it to you in a hash-house. But then if you were in a fancy restaurant with a tablecloth you probably wouldn't be mad enough to be pulling this trick. Now slide the paper out from under the glass (figure 3). Two or three drops of water may spill out, but don't

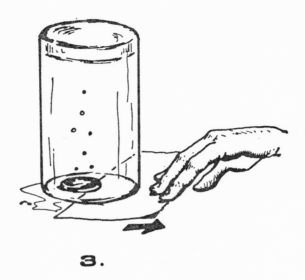

3.

worry. What you have left is a nickel tip inside an inverted glass of water.

There is no way to get the nickel out, or even to pick up the glass, without spilling the water. When the counter-man sees what you have done he will be angry, and you know how tough countermen are, so learn to perform this technique fast and get out in a hurry. For additional injury and insult, instead of using a nickel drop in a small foreign coin of no value whatsoever; Austrian ten-groschen pieces are perfect.

Part Two:
High, Wide and Handy

THE GRAND
RUBBER BAND MYSTERY

Long ago, everybody lived on farms, and the handiest way to show off was by walking up and down in front of the house on top of the picket fence. Nowadays, of course, nobody lives on farms any more; everybody lives in offices. Picket fences everywhere have been replaced by wire mesh, which is just about impossible to walk on top of; but offices are full of dandy furniture for showing off with.

Take, for example, the humble rubber band. (Of course if you do still live on a farm, or even in an ordinary house, you should still be able to find some kind of rubber band.) Anyhow, your object is, first, to wrap the rubber band inextricably around the fingers; second, to extricate the whole mess in a dazzling flash that nobody can understand. In fact, though we can show you how to do it, we don't profess to understand it ourselves. Just follow the directions, bearing in mind that all the illustrations are shown from your own point of view, not that of an observer.

Stick out your index finger (we show the left index

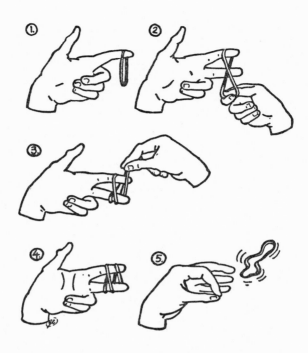

finger, because it's easier for most people to use the right hand to work on the left) and hang a rubber band on it (figure 1).

Grab the rubber band with your right hand and rotate it one-half turn to the right, as shown in figure 2.

Draw the rubber band—both halves of it—with your right hand away and below under your middle finger and wrap it round your index finger again, exactly as shown in figure 3. It's easy to go wrong here, but there's only one way to go wrong, so follow the drawing carefully, and if when you get to the end this doesn't work, go back and do it the other way. When you've finished the wrapping, the whole business should look like figure 4.

Now comes the dazzling flash. Close your thumb on the tip of your index finger. Obviously there is now no way in the world to get the rubber band off your hand.

However, you have only to wiggle your middle finger for a bit and zowie, the rubber band flies free (figure 5). Don't ask us why. Sometimes the rubber band will hang up on the middle finger, but if snapped briskly and with a perky enough band it will fly halfway across the room. Don't ask us how, either. Just rejoice that nobody else will ever be able to figure it out, no matter how many times you repeat it. It drives them crazy, and that's where the show-off wants them to be.

SNUFFING A CIGARETTE ON A FINE SILK SCARF

There are many places to show off with this trick. We suggest you sit in a fancy French restaurant and wait for a rich beautiful woman to walk by. If you're lucky, she'll drop her St. Laurent scarf at your feet. Reach down and pick it up, stub out your cigarette on it, then hand it back with a smile. The ice has been broken and you've impressed the heck out of the woman. We'll tell you here how it's done; learning how to smile is up to you.

While waiting for the beautiful woman to show up, take a half-dollar from your pocket and hold it in the palm of your hand. Make sure it is in the center of your palm (figure 1). (The coin will conduct the heat through the fabric, leaving the fabric undamaged.)

Now the woman walks by and drops the scarf. Pick it up with your free hand and wave it in the air with a flourish. This will make her realize there are no cigarette burns on the scarf to begin with. It will also remove attention from the hand holding the coin. Transfer the scarf to the hand with the coin. Open your fingers and place the scarf over your palm (figure 2).

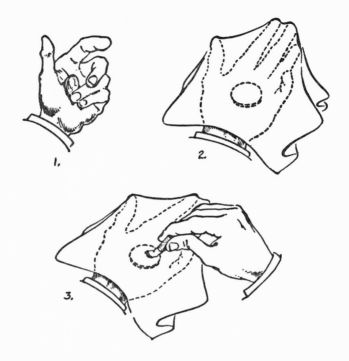

If the coin should slip out of your hand, abandon everything; you could wind up burning yourself. Just hand the scarf back, remembering not to blush. If all goes well, however, flick the loose ashes off the cigarette. A clean butt is of utmost importance; lingering bits of fire will burn holes. Now stub out the cigarette on the coin in three or four confident taps (figure 3).

Before you hand back the scarf, whisk it off the hand with the coin and shake it briskly. This will remove any remaining ashes from the scarf. The scarf has suffered no damage. If, though, you missed the coin and burned the scarf, offer to pay for it. A show-off is never a cheapskate.

CUTTING THE DECK WITH ONE HAND

If you like movies such as "The Sting," you'll love knowing how to cut the deck with one hand. You're sitting at the table with some sharpie on your right, a fellow who blows perfect smoke rings from a long, thin cheroot. He places the deck before you with disdain. You pause, then slowly extend your hand and pick it up. Bam! Bam! You slice the fifty-two with one hand—and not while the deck is still resting on the table. Want to know how to pull this off? Well, as promised, here's how:

Pick up the deck with your most trusted hand and turn it over, as shown in figure 1. Hold the deck with your thumb and the tips of your fingers. Keep your fingers fairly straight.

Holding the deck in place with your thumb, move the knuckle of your thumb out so that about half the cards drop down to your palm (figure 2). Before going further, practice this move until you can do it smoothly.

With the tip of your index finger, push the bottom half of the deck up toward your thumb (figure 3). Imagine that the cards are hinged at the heel of your hand—this will enable you to go only as far as you must. Open your hand slightly and, while holding the bottom half of the deck between your index. finger and thumb, let the top half slide down over your index finger (figure 4). Now all you have to do is close your thumb and you will have the full cut deck, as well as a psychological edge on your opponents.

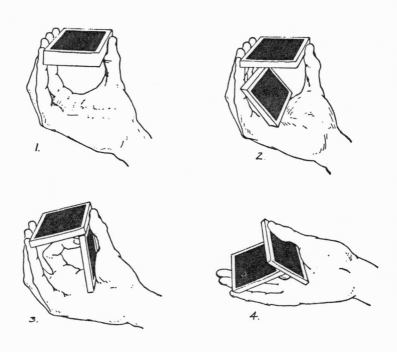

1.

2.

3.

4.

THE CLASSIC DECK FLIP

A deck of cards yields more hours of fun and profit than any other thing in the world, including the opposite sex. We could give you a new card trick every day for years—and never run out. But since we are committed to teaching you as many different ways to show off as is super-humanly possible, we'll try to restrain ourselves to just demonstrating one of the easiest, yet most impressive, maneuvers with a deck—spreading the fifty-two along your arm, then flipping the whole mess over.

Pick up a deck of cards with your right hand and, gently, so you don't blow the whole routine, squeeze the top and the bottom of the deck as shown in figure 1.

Stick out your left arm, firm but relaxed, making sure it extends in a straight line out from your shoulder. The palm of your hand should be slightly above your shoulder, but the rest of your arm should be straight as, well, an arrow.

Now, take the deck in your right hand and carefully beginning about an inch over your fingers, let the cards drop all the way up to your elbow (figure 2). They should flip forth smoothly, though practice will guarantee that they don't buzz all over the room, which would make you look like a real silly.

Here's the clincher. Your goal is to flip all the cards over in one magnificent domino effect. The best way to achieve this is to simply but decisively close your middle fingers, over which the first card is lying (figure 3). Do it! If your arm is still straight and firm, the whole deck should respond as though of a single mind.

Experts have come up with a number of interesting finales. You are welcome to experiment all you want, but here is the easiest (though still impressive): let your arm drop and the cards will slip down to your hand into one neat, orderly deck.

WARNING: If you perform this trick before sitting down to a friendly or not-so friendly card game, know full well you might scare everyone off before the first hand.

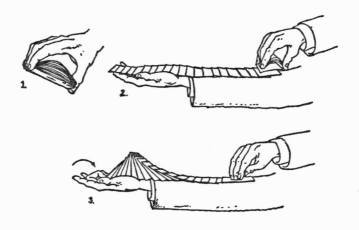

POP GOES THE BRACELET

This little manipulative technique drives people crazy to watch, but even crazier if they try it themselves. And they will try it themselves, because, unlike true tricks of sleight-of-hand, it is all done in the open and looks easy. Even if you have the ability to palm coins and make cigarettes disappear into thin air, you'll find it difficult to make people try to imitate your performance because they know they can't; whereas the bracelet pop conceals nothing, and therefore attracts the suckers to attempt to do likewise. Nothing establishes the superiority of the show-off faster.

All you need for the bracelet pop is two hands and a bracelet. The bracelet should be made of some plastic or metal that won't break when dropped, because dropping it in a spectacular way is what you intend to do. Don't try it with a wrist watch. In fact, the bracelet pop should only be performed over a table or similar surface to stop the fall. Here's how, now (please note that figures 1 through 4 are drawn from the point-of-view of the performer):

1. Loop the bracelet over your forefinger and rotate it

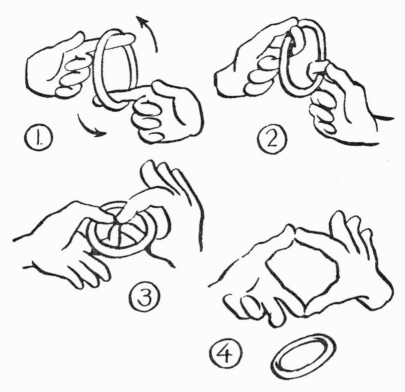

for a while by twirling your fingers in the direction shown in figure 1. If you find twirling in this direction awkward, twirl in the opposite direction; it doesn't make the slightest difference.

2. Stop twirling when your right hand is low and your left high, as shown in figure 2, and close the fingers and thumbs of your hands firmly on each other around the bracelet. The bracelet itself should remain loose; be sure not to pinch it.

3. Bring your hands together as shown in figure 3, with the thumbs and forefingers all touching in the center of the bracelet. Notice, however, that the tip of the right forefinger is adjacent to and touching the tip of the left thumb, and the tip of the left forefinger makes contact

with the tip of the right thumb. Got it?

4. Open your hands exactly as shown in figure 4, with the tips of the opposite forefingers and thumbs firmly pressed together. The bracelet falls free. What's so amazing about that, you ask. Well, the answer is that the faster and more gracefully you do it the more amazing it becomes, because, to all appearances, the bracelet passes right through, not between, your fingers. Where, after all, did you let go? You appear to have had a firm grip on it ever since step 2, yet, flip! there it goes. After a little practice, you'll find it simple to do all four steps so quickly that the spin imparted to the bracelet in step 1 stays with it, and it pops out smartly and rolls away.

What's more, for some reason even a show-off can't explain, the motion of the bracelet pop is very difficult to follow; imitators almost always wind up with the wrong fingers against the wrong thumbs, and the bracelet firmly locked in place. For you it works, for them it won't; and a show-off can ask for no greater sense of superiority.

THE RING AND THE STRING

The virtue of this little beauty lies in its use of everyday materials to produce an effect totally beyond the comprehension of the observer. In fact, we're not so sure we comprehend it ourselves, but we're going to show you how it's done all the same; then you can figure it out at leisure. What happens is, you thread a loop of string through the middle of a ring (or anything else with a hole in it) and ask someone to hold the string on his fingers (figure 1). Then, by a few deft manipulations, you remove the ring from the string, without ever lifting the string off the fingers! Obviously this is impossible, so don't trouble your mind about trying to figure it out; show-offs have more important things to think about. Just follow the instructions and take the credit. Here's how:

Leaving the ring in about the middle of the strings, reach over the near string with the left hand, grasp the far string, and pull it toward you over the top of the near string (figure 2).

Now, with your right hand, reach underneath the string you are holding in your left hand. Grab the remain-

49

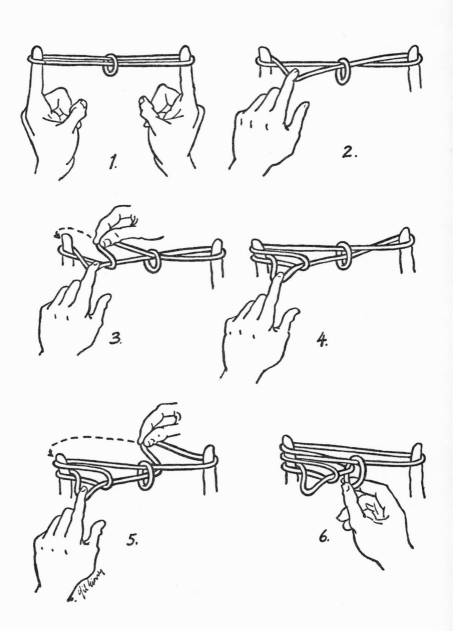

ing string—the one you are not holding in your left hand—a little to the right of the left hand, and pull the string toward you. Pull out some slack, and loop it once around your victim's right index finger (left from your point of view) (figure 3), and let go with the right hand, but keep holding on to the string in your left (figure 4).

Next, with your right hand reach over the near string on the right side of the ring, grab the far string, and pull it into another loop over the right (left, as we said, from your point of view) index finger of the patsy (figure 5). Don't let go with the left hand yet! And don't worry about where the ring has slid to by now.

Finally, grab the ring with your right hand. Let go of the string in your left hand. Pull gently on the ring (figure 6). The strings will all slide around a little bit and the ring will be free. If you don't believe us, just try it.

Now you know the fundamentals; variations are up to your ingenuity. Gilt string from Christmas wrappings makes the whole trick particularly tasteful; or if your style of showing off calls for gigantism, you might want to use a big piece of rope and a bicycle tire.

THE PEARL OF INDIA
AFFINITY TEST

You are having lunch or dinner with a beautiful lady. You tell her that by virtue of your mystic powers you can determine whether she is your true soul-mate. If she's still listening, you invite her to participate in an ancient mystic rite of India. It is, of course, quite decent. What you need, you say, is a priceless pearl and a beaker of acid, but since you are having lunch, a cube of sugar and a glass of water will do. You hand the beautiful creature the cube of sugar, and invite her to draw on it, with a pen, a clear and simple design—say, a heart with your initial on it. You take the cube of sugar, flourish it, and drop it into a glass of water, or a cup of coffee. The cube of sugar is now gone, destroyed right? Right. Now, for the grand finale and most impressive effect ever, you invite her to concentrate for a few seconds on the palms of her hands; then to hold her hands directly over the glass of water and concentrate a few seconds longer. Then you say: "Turn your hands over." And there, big as life, on one palm, is the exact design she drew on the cube of sugar! And yet the cube, which she never touched, is under water dissolving. She is yours!

Now, how is this done? Let's go back to the design on the sugar (figure 1). This must be clear, simple and in ink. If it's not clear and simple enough, tell her the spirits don't like it and ask for another.

When the spirits are satisfied, pick up a glass of ice water with your left hand and move it to the center of the table. The ostensible purpose of this move is ceremonial; the real purpose is to dampen your thumb slightly from the condensation on the outside of the glass. Then, when you pick up the sugar cube and say the magic word *mekkamussulmannenmonumentenmacher,* the design will be transferred to your damp and slightly sticky thumb—provided, of course, you have your thumb square on the design (figure 2). The rest is child's play; when she holds her hands over the glass with the sugar, help her adjust their position. Press the palm of her hand, which of course is facing down over the glass, just once with your thumb (figure 3). Don't smear! The design is now transferred. Now it's up to you to get your thumb out of the way without being spotted, carry on with the hocus-pocus for a few more seconds, and ask her to turn over. Perfect! Now just don't forget *mekkamussulmannenmonumenten-macher,* but if you forget it anyhow, try *abracadabra.*

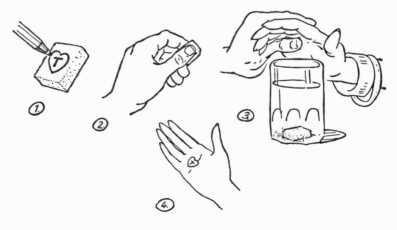

WHISTLING THROUGH GRASS

Going out into the fields and meadows is supposed to be relaxing, but the true show-off never misses an opportunity. A classic pastoral attention-grabber is whistling through a blade of grass. Many of you probably know how to do this, while more of you have doubtless seen and heard it performed. For those of you who have somehow missed the boat, here's all there is to it.

But first, *when* do you whistle through grass? Our opinion is that you wait until it's very quiet, when the only sounds you hear are the sweet chirping of crickets and the melodic strains of birds in the trees. Then you pluck a blade, place it between your hands, and blow. The crickets and birds will fall at your feet, deeply in awe.

Pick a blade of grass around six inches long. Hold it between your thumb and index finger. With your other hand, pull the blade tight against the thumb holding it (figure 1).

Keep the edge of the blade facing you. The point is to have as narrow a surface as possible close to your mouth. The best position is shown in figure 2.

Place your left thumb against your right thumb. Your hands come together in two places: at the thumbs' first knuckles and at the ball of the hand below each thumb. Make sure to lock the blade in at these two points; keep the blade as rigid as possible (figure 3).

Now blow steadily, not too strong, not too weak. Practice until you get a smooth, confident sound. Once you master this trick you'll never forget it. It's like swimming and riding a bicycle.

There are a number of other great stunts you can pull off in the woods. But don't expect us to teach you these. This, remember, is family entertainment.

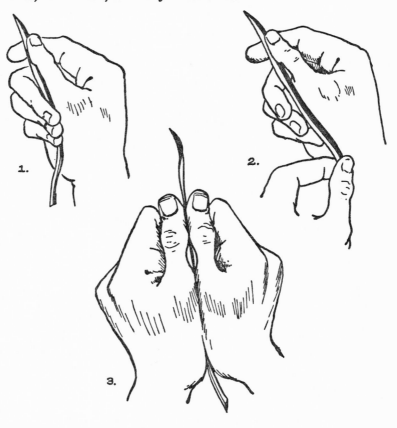

THE TRUTH BEHIND
THE FALSE KNOT

Tying a false knot is a familiar part of the magician's stock in trade. With a little rehearsal, however, it can be done by anyone, even a klutz. All you need is a piece of rope a few feet long. Mom, you can impress the neighbors when you're outside hanging clothes on the line. Dad, you might try to amaze your buddies on a fishing trip. Kids, well, you can show off with a rope anywhere you like. Here is how to tie a "tight knot," then make it disappear in a flash.

Hold the rope between the extended second and third fingers of your left hand; press down on the rope with the ring and little fingers of this hand. Hold the other end of the rope with the thumb and fingers of your right hand (figure 1).

Take the end in your right hand and cross it over your left hand—over the point where your ring and little fingers are holding down their end of the rope. Droop it over your left hand and let it rest next to your thumb (point A in figure 2). Now, with your free hand, reach for the end of the rope marked B. You are going to pull this end through

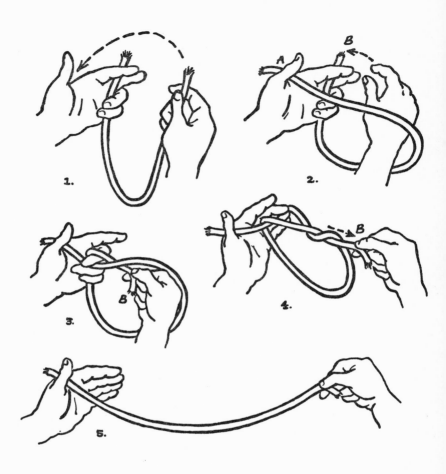

the loop you've created, but not until you introduce the sneaky little maneuver that follows.

As you are pulling end B through the loop, bend the middle finger of your left hand and draw back a little loop in the opposite direction (figure 3). This second loop is a slip knot; without it, your big knot will not come apart.

Once your slip knot has been made, pull end B to form a tight knot (figure 4). But be careful not to yank on it too hard or too fast. What you want to do is stop before the knot comes apart. Practice will tell you when.

Now here's the punch line. You may either pull both ends of the rope to make the knot vanish, or you may run your hand across the rope, removing it that way. Try it both ways and see which one gives you the greater feeling of importance.

All this seems more complicated than it really is. You should get the hang of it after two or three tries.

AN OLD SWITCHEROO

Showing off can be divided into two main kinds of behavior. The first consists of doing things that are spectacular in themselves, like riding a bicycle "no-hands." The second is made up of doing things that nobody else can do, no matter how dumb the things are in themselves, like, for instance, card tricks. There isn't any earthly reason for card tricks, but that doesn't stop audiences from gaping enthusiastically at the simplest sleights. Likewise, the only reason for learning the Old Switcheroo is because once you know it, you'll find that nobody else can figure it out.

Here's what you do: you pick up a couple of small cylindrical objects in the forks of your thumbs, as shown in figure 1. Corks are good, and so are lipsticks or 35-millimeter film cans.

Then, holding one in each hand, you proceed to do the following impossible thing. Grasp the left-hand cork, or whatever you are using, between the thumb and fingers of your right hand. At the same time, grasp the right-hand cork between the thumb and fingers of your left hand. Finally, with a twist of the wrist, separate the hands

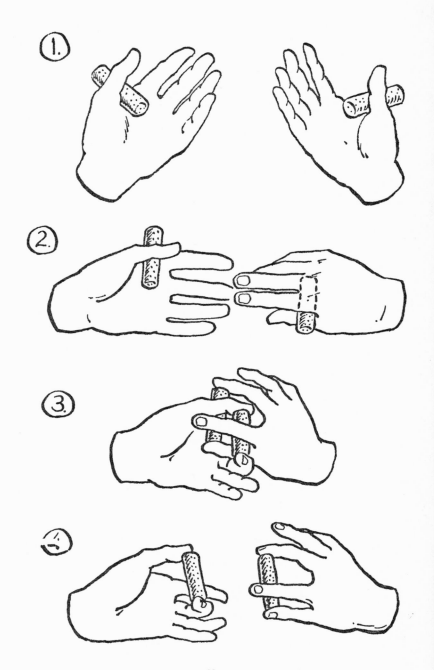

1.

2.

3.

4.

without letting go of the corks. Does that sound easy? If it does, just try it at this point without reading the rest of the instructions.

To do it right, go back to figure 1. Now, rotate your right hand palm-down, as shown in figure 2.

Now, bring your hands together (figure 3), with the right hand above the left. Keep the two corks parallel to each other. Grasp the corks exactly as shown. Apparently the fingers and corks are inextricably tangled-up together, and that's the beauty of the trick; in actual fact they aren't interlocked at all, as we shall presently see.

Now, you can simply draw your hands apart, as shown in figure 4. But it's much more impressive to give a little twist of the wrists before doing so, because a half-turn or so obscures the action and gives the illusion that the corks have passed right through each other.

Keep repeating this action until you can do it smoothly and swiftly. Then go out and challenge someone you know to do the same. Unless you deliberately explain step-by-step, you'll have him sweating and straining and red with rage as he cobbles up his fingers something awful trying to solve it.

MASTERING
THE FRENCH DROP

This is a splendidly versatile trick of magic that will serve you until death. You've seen it a zillion times; some people use coins, others ping-pong balls. As long as an object fits neatly into your palm, it's a good drop prop. The trick is this: you make something disappear into thin air, then reproduce it. It's easy to do but not so easy for an audience to figure out.

Hold a coin, say a quarter, between the thumb and index finger of your left hand. Use the tips of these two fingers exclusively, as in figure 1.

Slowly pass the thumb of your right hand under the coin in a smooth, even motion, as in figure 2.

You want to give the impression that this right hand is actually taking the coin. But instead of transferring the coin, you let it drop from the thumb and index finger into the palm of the left hand. Figure 3 shows the dropping of the coin. Keep the fingers of your left hand between the coin and the person watching you. In this way, the dropping of the coin is entirely concealed.

Now, to really hook your audience, present a closed

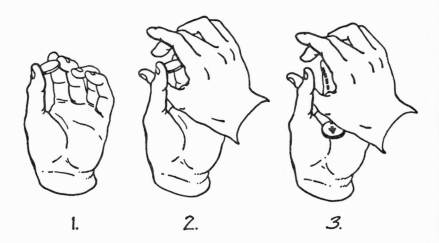

1.   2.   3.

right fist. This tells the onlooker you have "obviously" transferred the coin. Ask the chump to blow, tap, or otherwise activate some magical power on your right hand. Then open your fingers dramatically. Huh? Where did it go?

Now some possible grand finales. Put your left hand, the one still holding the coin, to the sucker's ear and pretend to pull the coin out of his ear. Or pull it out of your ear. Or your mouth. Get the point?

FOUR IMPRESSIVE
SHADOW PICTURES

Anybody can deface a wall with spray paint, but while the graffiti artist may think he's a big shot, he's really just a cheap shot. When you're faced with a nice clean wall and nothing to do, don't be dumb and destructive, be classy and creative.

Shadow pictures are easily learned and very impressive. All you need is a source of concentrated light and a white wall or screen. One of the best light sources is a slide or movie projector. Try showing off with shadow pictures after you've shown shots of your last vacation and bored everybody silly. Here are four terrific designs with which to start your repertoire. After you've mastered them, try coming up with some of your own (fat chance, right?).

Figure 1—The Flying Dove

This is one of the basic designs. To get the dove moving, flap your fingers gracefully.

Figure 2—The Black Rabbit

There are three moving parts here: wiggle your top fingers to make his ears twitch; move the middle, ring, and little fingers of your bottom hand to get him sniffing and

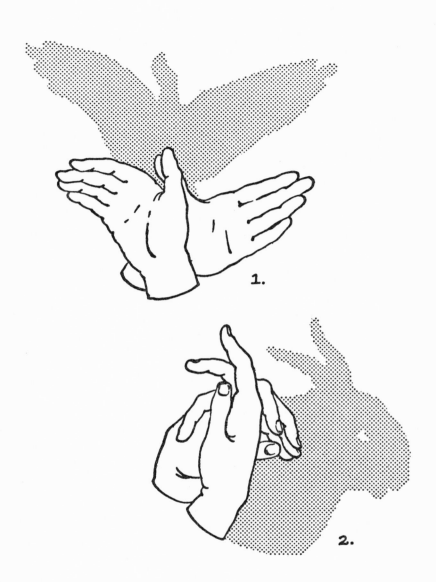

1.

2.

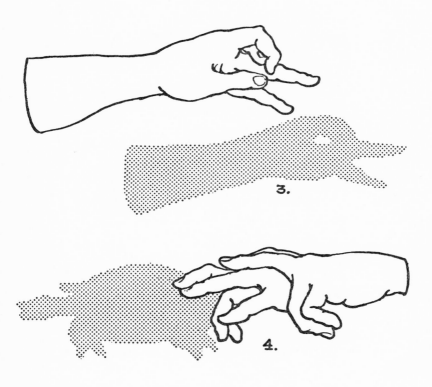

3.

4.

chomping; close your hand slightly to make him blink.

Figure 3—Mother Goose

You'll have to roll up your sleeves for this (unless you want your goose to look like she's wearing a collar). Close your ring and little fingers to get her squawking.

Figure 4—Mr. Tortoise

This one's a bit tougher to master, but keep trying. You can make his head sway and go into his shell. But are you smart enough to figure out how?

ROLLING A COIN
ACROSS YOUR KNUCKLES

You've seen this beauty a hundred times in the movies: a cowboy in a white hat stands by the corral just as cool and tough as can be. He takes out a coin, smiles a little, then stands there rolling the coin across his knuckles, first one way, then back again. You can do it while waiting to buy popcorn at the movies, or on the corner waiting for a bus. It will make you feel like a young John Wayne. Here's how to roll a quarter or a half-dollar across the top of your knuckles.

Don't use any coin smaller than a quarter, it's rough doing with a penny or a nickel. Moisten your middle knuckles with your tongue; this will help keep the coin from slipping. Place the coin on the side of your thumb, as shown in figure 1.

Hold the coin on your thumb until you feel relaxed. Now carefully flip it onto your index-finger knuckle so that the coin hangs over the knuckle on the middle-finger side. If it does not hang in this direction the trick won't work (figure 2).

Extend your fingers and keep your muscles stiff. Drop

your index finger and raise your middle finger simultaneously (figure 3). Your middle finger should touch down on the coin, forcing it up onto the middle finger. Hold it now. Okay. Do the same thing to move the coin to your third finger.

When the coin is between your third finger and pinky, you have the option to proceed in one of two ways. You can palm the coin and bring it back to your thumb for another crossing, or you can flip it back across your knuckles in the opposite direction. To do this, follow the above instructions, only in reverse (figure 4).

Word of warning: since mostly tough guys or con-men use the coin roll in real life, it's a good idea to give some thought to where you might be seen trying it. Two additional safe places are the supermarket check-out line and the laundromat. Don't try it in places inhabited by punks or bullies—unless you can also roll them across your knuckles.

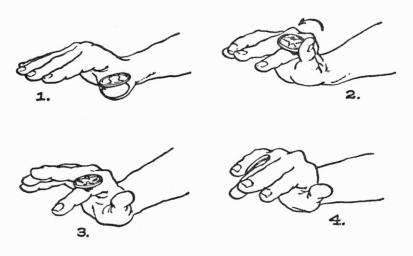

DO-IT-YOURSELF
DECAPITATION

Stage magicians like to tell you that the hand is quicker than the eye. Like everything else about stage magicians, this proposition is illusory, as you know if you've ever practiced a sleight-of-hand trick and then had it fail because the audience just can't seem to keep from watching you very carefully.

The truth is, the professional magician succeeds where you fail because he has the power to direct your attention somewhere else while he is reaching up his sleeve for the rabbit. Now, cutting off your head with a piece of string depends upon a ridiculously simple manipulation of the string. Anybody who actually sees what you are doing will see right through the trick. But this is the case with almost every sleight-of-hand. What we're showing you is not only how to do the trick, but how to conceal it, which is harder.

Tie a piece of ordinary string into a loop. Somewhat less than a yard of string should make a loop about the right size. Exhibit the string so anybody can see it's genuine solid string. Put your thumbs in the loop and pull

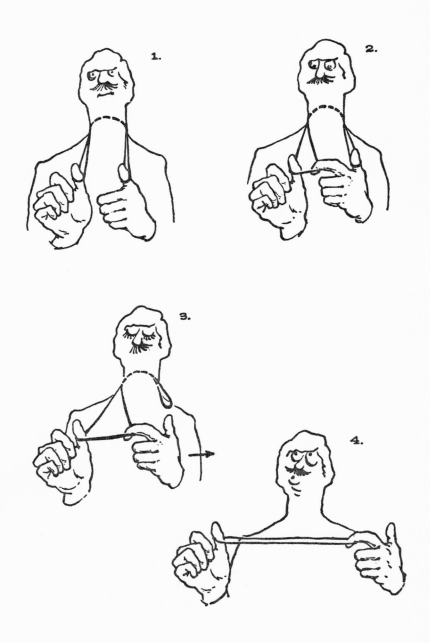

it around your neck (see figure 1).

Announce that you're about to cut off your head with a piece of string. Now this is what you do to distract attention: say something like "Now the string is going to pass directly through my neck. Please examine my neck. You can see there is no slot or passage from one side to the other. You will see that my neck is perfectly solid."

As you say this, turn your back. As you turn your back, bring your hands, and the ends of the loop of string, together in front of you. While your back is still turned, stick your right index finger into the left end of the loop (figure 2). Keep the loop taut with both thumbs, and (this is very important) keep talking all the time about the back of your neck. As you reach the end of your patter, do three things at the same time:

1. turn back to face the audience while

2. removing the right thumb from the right end of the loop, while

3. pulling the loop around the left side of your neck, supported by your left thumb and your right index finger (figure 3). If you do this smartly, the loop will appear to pass right through your neck.

Quickly hold up the loop in front of you to show that it is unbroken (figure 4). Then hand it immediately to a spectator before somebody observes that the string is now looped, not between your thumbs, but between a thumb and an index finger. Shake your head to show that it doesn't fall off.

Remember two very important things: Never do the same trick twice, or somebody will see through it; and always find a way to get the audience to look somewhere else. Professional magicians distract the audience with showmanship, which requires talent; we've shown you how to do it by putting your back between the audience and the gimmick, which only requires nerve. Remember, the point of showing off is to look better, smarter and more highly skilled than in fact you are.

SPARE CHANGE?

Times being what they are, you probably don't have as much change in your pocket as you used to. That is, except if you have an oil well buried in your back yard. Not long ago, we met a fellow who has quite a few of them—and there was the clanking of coins in his robe to prove it. We chatted a while about the world situation, then the fellow produced some quarters and performed a feat that left us speechless. We are still speechless. So speechless, in fact, that we will let our chic sheik teach you the trick himself.

HERE'S A NEAT
LITTLE NUMBER
YOU CAN DO
WITH JUST SOME
SPARE CHANGE

BALANCE ONE OR MORE COINS ON YOUR ELBOW LIKE THIS THEN...

...IN ONE SWIFT MOVE YOU BRING YOUR FOREARM FORWARD AND CATCH THEM ALL. NOW OFFER THE COINS TO A FOLLOWER TO DO THE SAME.

HE, OF COURSE WILL SPRAY THE COINS ALL OVER THE TENT—NOT KNOWING IT'S NECESSARY TO BEND THE KNEES AS YOU ARE MAKING YOUR MOVE.

TWO TRICKS FOR A BUCK

Everyone talks about the shrinking dollar but nobody does anything about it. We will! Right now we'll show you how to get years of great entertainment out of a dollar bill—and it won't cost you a red cent!

We learned this feat from a show-off named Marjorie. It seems that for years she has been conspiring with her brother-in-law at family get-togethers. The brother-in-law, playing the straight man, says, "Let's see Marjorie cut a pencil in two with a dollar bill." Then Marjorie, a great entertainer if there ever was one, does just that. Here is how she does it.

Take a dollar bill, preferably a new, stiff one, and hold it in whichever hand is most comfortable. Fold the bill neatly in half, lengthwise, as shown in figure 1. Now have someone hold a full-size lead pencil at each end with the thumb and forefinger. Tell him to hold the pencil about a foot in front of his body. And tell him to hold the pencil as tightly as possible.

With the hand holding the bill, extend your index finger so it looks like you're using it to keep the bill straight. But after you lift the bill in the air, and just before you strike it against the pencil, extend your index finger. It is the finger that actually cracks the pencil in two, not the bill. But the finger is hidden within the folds of the dollar bill and is never detected. Figure 2 shows the correct position of the finger within the bill.

Now for the second part of this twofer, a classic show-off maneuver. We'll try this one out on you. Take a dollar bill and find the mushroom in it. That's right, there's a mushroom to be found on every American buck. Check the front of the bill, now the back. Find it yet? No? Want to know where it is? We'll give you a clue—it can be found by folding George Washington's forehead down over his frilly shirt front. See? Yuk, yuk.

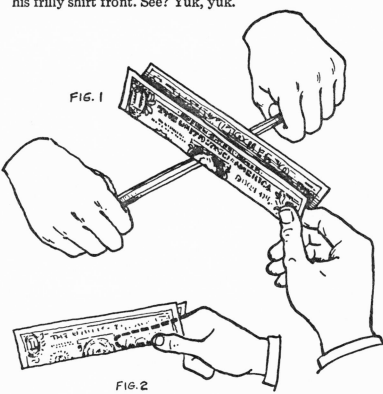

FIG. 1

FIG. 2

OFF WITH YOUR THUMB!

Going though life with our members intact is a goal we all share; but there are advantages to some detachable parts. Some day you may choose to sacrifice your toupee to save your life from wild Indians or, when exploring the Amazon basin, impress the natives with your strength and agility by popping your false teeth in and out. Even harsher measures have been tried; Vincent Van Gogh cut off one ear to please a lady, and went even crazier than he was when that didn't work.

A much safer arrangement, which has the virtue of being both painless and reversible, is to learn how to pull your thumb off and put it back at will. Before you go any further, we'd better make it perfectly clear—but only to you—that this is nothing but an illusion. Your thumb will only *appear* to come off. But that's your secret and ours—to the world at large, you will appear to be the detachable-thumb champion of the world.

A word of caution first: this trick has been known to make children cry and weak women faint, so watch it, because you don't want to be responsible for anybody's

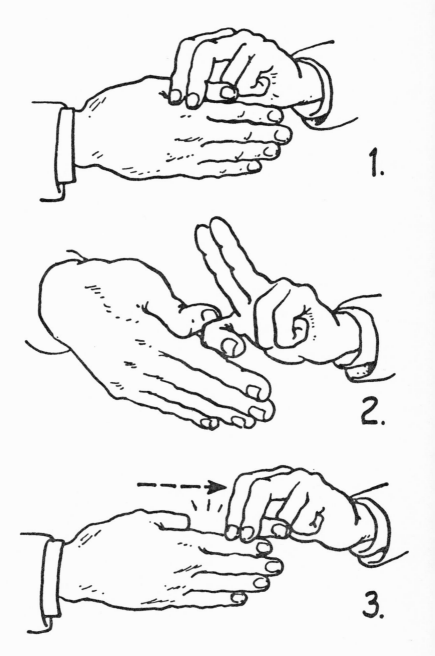

emotional condition but your own. But enough of the sincerity, just practice the following steps:

1. Present your left hand, covering the first joint of your left thumb with the first two fingers of your right hand, as in figure 1. It's a little hard to get attention in this position—you can't wave your hands around—so you may have to clear your throat and say something arresting like "Wanna see my old war wound?" or "I bet Robert Redford can't do this!" Hesitate a moment and check your positioning. Figure 2 shows the actual position of fingers and thumbs. Bend the left thumb as far out of the way as you can get it.

3. Pull your right hand to the left, taking with it what appears to be the end of your left thumb. Some pull it off with a mighty roar and an appearance of great effort, but in our opinion this detracts from the effect; the best way is to just nonchalantly slide the thing off. Then, before anybody has a chance to figure out what you're up to, slide it back on.

Pick up any fainting women from the floor, and try to soothe the weeping children, but be sure not to do the same stunt before the same audience another time, no matter how much they ask you. People will catch on, and the great object of a life like ours is to always keep them guessing.

CRUSHING A BEER CAN
WITH YOUR BARE HAND

We are talking here about a steel beer can, not that new aluminum kind. Aluminum is for sissies, and everybody knows it.

Contrary to popular belief, crushing a beer can with one hand does not require strength. Brute strength will do it, sure, but the point of showing off is to do more and better things than your natural endowments allow (which is probably not much to begin with). Properly done, the trick lies in the technique.

Why crush beer cans? you might wonder. First, it flattens them and keeps them from rolling noisily down church or railroad-car aisles. More important, crushing beer cans is a terrific way to get attention on the beach or at a fraternity party. Extra points are won by laying waste to a vast number of cans throughout an afternoon or evening. Remember that you yourself must drink the beer from all cans you endeavor to crush. Don't go around picking up other people's cans. It simply doesn't look good. Ready now?

1. Hold the can in whichever hand is most comfort-

able. The ends of the can should be equidistant from the point at which the can rests on your palm (figure 1).

2. Place your middle finger on the can's midpoint and squeeze firmly with the middle finger, backed up with the third and index fingers (figure 2). Make a slight dent, but be careful not to dent the opposite, palm side of the can.

3. Deepen the crease until it is about one-third of the can's diameter. The crease should be perpendicular to the length of the can and equidistant from each end. As you deepen the crease, begin to rotate the can slightly (figure 3).

4. Exert more force with your fingers. Keep it up until the valley of the crease is a quarter-inch from the palm side of the can (which should still be smooth and unbuckled). Now, shifting your grip if necessary, squeeze the ends of the can toward each other until the can begins to fold up (figure 4).

5. Push the ends of the can together until they touch (figure 5).

Practice the procedure until it all takes but a few seconds. If there is a trash barrel nearby, throw the crushed can into it. Don't litter—being a slob is never a way to make a good impression.

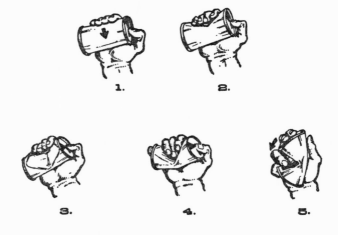

1. 2.

3. 4. 5.

WHISTLING
WITH TWO FINGERS

Whistling with two fingers is a sure way to get the attention of taxis, horses and dogs. It produces a shriller, more impressive noise than whistling without fingers. It also looks nicer, and gives the whistler more authority, because if you whistle without fingers people may not notice that you are the source of the earsplitting racket. Here's how:

1. Place the tips of your forefingers together (figure 1). Some people use four fingers, though the principle is the same. The four-finger technique employs the middle and index finger of each hand.

2. Keeping the fingertips together, place them just under the tip of your tongue and raise it slightly. Push the tongue backward until your lips close on the first knuckles of your fingers (figure 2). When mastering this step, use a mirror (but make sure you're alone).

3. Tighten your lips over your fingers and against your teeth until there is no way that air can escape except through the sound-box created in the V between the ends of your fingers (figure 3).

4. This anatomical drawing shows the correct position of fingers, lips and tongue. Now blow steadily. Move your fingertips back and fourth until you hear that first wonderful chirp.

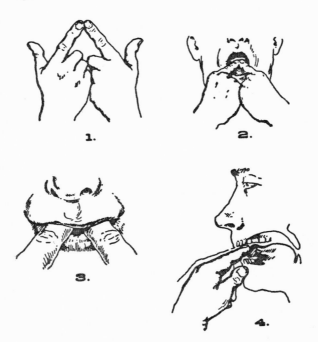

HOW TO BE VERY,
VERY INCOMBUSTIBLE

A show-off rarely or never goes to cocktail parties. There are many excellent reasons for this reluctance, some social (cocktail parties are boring), some moral (cocktail parties are wicked), some medical (tobacco, alcohol and talking too loud are bad for your health sooner or later). But the most important reason for staying away is egotistical: eventually everybody at a cocktail party starts showing off, and that means it's going to be hard for you to get the attention you deserve. Your message will become lost and fuzzed in the social static.

Nevertheless, suppose that, much against your will, you find yourself at a cocktail party with one of those cold things in your hand and somebody blowing cigarette smoke into your earholes. What you have to do is make the best of it, and the best you can make of it is to show yourself not only sober but fireproof. Politely but aggressively you approach the man or woman with the cigarette and ask: "What is that thing you're smoking?"

"Why, it's a Brand X," he/she replies.

"May I see it?" you inquire in a winning voice.

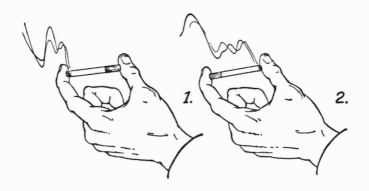

"Of course," is the response you anticipate. What you do next is, you pick the cigarette up between your thumb and forefinger, as shown in figure 1, and you just hold it for a while. Then you turn it around and hold it the other way round (figure 2). Then after you've made your point, you hand it back.

Now, how did you do this without getting burned? Easy. Remember the cold thing in your hand? It was a glass full of ice and something, no doubt. You held it for a long time—maybe fifteen minutes, until your fingertips were very cold. Every time your fingers warmed the spot on the glass beneath them, you rotated the glass to a fresh cold place. What's more, the condensation on the glass coated your fingers with a film of water. Only when your fingertips were thoroughly chilled did you venture to pick up the hot coal of the cigarette—and because the heat flow from the cigarette took a while to warm your fingers up to an uncomfortable temperature, you didn't get burned. In fact, if your fingers were damp enough, the cigarette just plain went out before you handed it back. That showed them, didn't it?

A word of warning: fire will burn if you overdo it. When you begin to feel the heat, get rid of the cigarette. Two or three seconds is plenty to prove that you're made of the very best asbestos.

Part Three:
Arts and Crafty

HOW TO MAKE
CUSTOM-MADE MONEY

In these hard times it is getting more and more difficult to have a lot of money. But it's easy to look like you
do. In fact, you can even give the impression that you have
your cash custom-made.

Go to the bank and get fifty new dollar bills, as crisp as
the bank can give you. Go home and make ready an empty
checkbook cover, preferably one with your name stamped
on the front. Also, make ready the empty cardboard that
once held the checks in place. Such a cardboard is shown
in figure 1.

Cut a strip of gauze to fit the edge of cardboard. Now,
with glue—we recommend rubber cement—coat the gauze
and adhere it to the edge of the cardboard, as in figure 2.

Keeping your stack of bills in a neat pile, carefully
stick them to the edge of the cardboard. Set aside to dry.
Then, insert the cardboard into your personalized cover
and close it.

All this comes in handy the next time you go up to a
cashier to pay a bill or check. Tear out the necessary
number of bills without giving the impression this is in any

way strange. You, God bless you, come out looking like one rich dude!

THE SHOW-OFF
PAPER AIRPLANE

Everybody knows how to make some kind of paper airplane. The difference between everybody and a show-off is that the show-off knows what a paper airplane is good for. The purpose of a paper airplane is not to fly well. As an aerodynamic vehicle, no paper airplane is very good and most are lousy. Those who, in spite of our advice, want to build paper airplanes that fly less badly than others may read and profit by *Scientific American's Great Paper Airplane Book,* available from your bookseller; but that's not, we repeat, the purpose of paper airplanes.

The purpose of paper airplanes is to attract attention and register boredom. Wherever a lot of people are gathered together working with paper, most of them aren't really working at all. What better way to annoy the few who are actually busy than by making and flying a truly elaborate paper airplane? In fact, it's better if you don't fly it, because that shows you're only making it because you have nothing better to do. For this purpose, the more elaborate the paper airplane the better, and here's the most elaborate we know. Just follow these few simple instructions, and you'll get a paper airplane that flies well enough if you really insist.

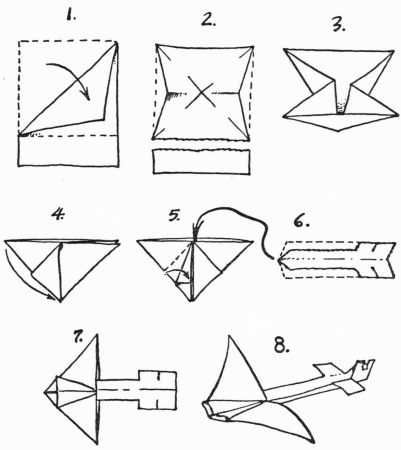

Take a piece of 8 1/2 by 11 inch typing paper and fold it diagonally to make a square (figure 1). Crease the portion that remains at the bottom and tear off, but do not discard. Crease the square along the opposite diagonal as well, then crease it straight across the middle (figure 2).

Fold the left and right sides together till they meet.

The end result of this step is a triangle with the point at the bottom, as shown in figure 3.

The triangle is really two layers thick. Take the top layer at one end and fold down to the point at the bottom, as shown on the left side of figure 4. Then repeat for the right side.

Fold one more time to the center, as shown on the left side of figure 5; repeat for the right side.

Now return to the extra strip you tore off in the beginning. Crease a V down its middle, then tear it into the shape shown in figure 6 to serve as the tail of the airplane. The pointed end at left should match the point at the bottom of the triangle as shown in figure 5.

Take the tail and stick it inside the triangle (we might as well call it the wing now) at the point shown in figure 5. Now the whole thing should look like figure 7.

Carefully keeping the tail in place, rip from the point of the nose backwards down the middle of the plane. Stop ripping when you have reached the front of the fat little subordinate triangles you made in step 5. Then take the nose, which is now torn into two sections, fold the sections back, and stuff them into those two little triangles. This gives you the blunt nose shown in the final illustration. Fold the tail as shown.

Now you have it. It adds stability to crease the wing just a little bit, giving it a slight dihedral angle. The plane may be glided softly out a high window, or for altitude you can hold it by the nose, placing your forefinger down the middle of the wing, and heave it; the tail collapses, but snaps back again when velocity drops at the height of the plane's trajectory. By now, if you've been following these instructions in your office, you've probably been fired. So just go on down to the nearest park and let fly.

GROWING A CARROT
UPSIDE DOWN

We all live now in the Golden Age of Houseplants. Ecological consciousness surrounds us from right and from left, and every windowsill in the nation is full of green growing stuff, from moss to mushrooms.

The showoff should, of course, have bigger and better house plants than other people, but how to grow house plants is itself a book-length subject we won't go into here (though we could, of course) so we trust you to look out for yourself mostly. We'll just have to be content with showing you how to grow a carrot upside down into a green and leafy little urn, suspended neatly in the window by a piece of string. We'll bet everybody else on your block grows his carrots right-side-up.

Get the biggest carrot you can find, and wash it nice and clean. Then lay it on the chopping block and neatly cut it off a convenient length from the green end (figure 1). Four or five inches should be enough except in the case of the largest carrots. Peel the other end and eat it.

Now, make a hole in your piece of carrot. Use any convenient kind of hole-maker; a woodworking bit of

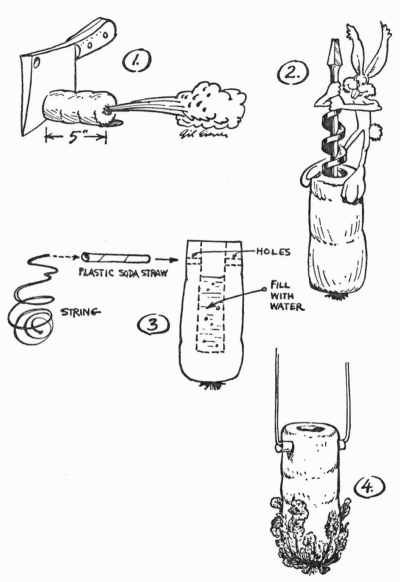

1.

← 5" →

Gil Evans

2.

3.

PLASTIC SODA STRAW

STRING

HOLES

FILL WITH WATER

4.

the right size, held in the hand, is about the neatest way (figure 2). Hole out your carrot until you have a cross-section like figure 3.

Punch a couple of holes an inch or so from the top (we are going to call the green end the bottom from now on) of the carrot, and thread a piece of string through. Hang it up in a sunny window. Fill up the carrot with water.

In a few days green things will begin to sprout (figure 4). In a few more days they will start to grow upward. In a couple of months, if you remember to keep turning the carrot around, they will grow into a sort of ferny green urn-shaped gob of foilage around the carrot.

The only things to watch out for are these: first, as your carrot grows more and more leaves it will require more and more water daily. Don't ever let it dry out. Second, the flesh of the carrot above water level is bound to wither some, and as it does the strings will begin cutting upwards from the holes you put them in. Eventually the carrot will be sliced through and you'll have to start with a fresh carrot, but you can delay this moment somewhat by lining the holes with pieces of plastic soda straw, or some kind of appropriate grommets, or something; you figure out what kind.

Finally, it probably won't hurt if once a month or so you mix up some soluble fertilizer. Follow the instructions on the package—only use about half as much as it says— and water the carrot with this instead of plain water.

THE NEWSPAPER TREE

If you read books, chances are you read newspapers, which is in itself a most enjoyable and educational experience. But what do you do when you're finished? Well, if everyone else in the family has read the paper, why not learn one of the great old tricks that needs as raw material only the paper itself? In case you don't know how, here is how to make a glorious tree out of a newspaper, which is better for the ecology than the other way around.

Using the full length of the paper, tear off two strips not less than ten or twelve inches wide. Then, with one inside the other and overlapping the other by a couple of inches, gently roll them up.

Take the rolled strips and, with a scissors or neatly with your fingers, make a series of incisions lengthwise, about five of them. Your roll should look like figure 2.

Make sure that your incisions come about midway down the roll. Your tree is now ready to sprout. This step, particularly if you're trying to impress children, should be executed with a grand flourish. Holding the uncut roll in one hand, use your other hand to take the center of the roll and pull up on it. Pull gently so you don't rip the roll or disturb the incisions. Your tree should look more or less like the tree in figure 3.

You can now use the rest of the paper to create an entire forest of trees, or simply plant the first in the corner of your room and watch to see if it grows. If it doesn't, try talking to it—some say that helps.

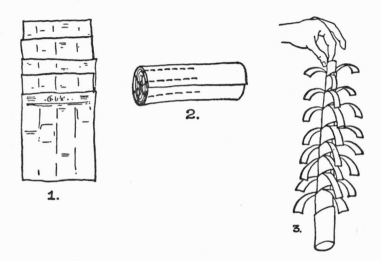

1.

2.

3.

SECRETS OF
THE WATER BOMB

When America was young and ingenious, college kids—and kids even younger than that—used to create, from mere pieces of paper, containers to fill with water and drop on each other from dormitory windows and other high places. Paper was used because milk bottles were heavy enough to be dangerous and rubber balloons were too expensive. Today, the wheel has come full circle—milk doesn't arrive in bottles, but in plastic or paper containers folded by vast impersonal machines. Return now to those thrilling days of yesteryear, and learn how to make a paper water-bomb; and when your destructive impulses are satisfied, you will find that with just a tug here and a pull there, the water-bomb snaps into a perfect cube, useful for building castles along the edge of your desk.

Start by folding a sheet of paper on its diagonal and cutting off the excess material to get a perfect square (figure 1). Crease the square thus obtained in both directions between corners (figure 2) and then collapse two opposite sides (not corners) inwards, toward each other, to obtain the triangular shape shown in figure 3.

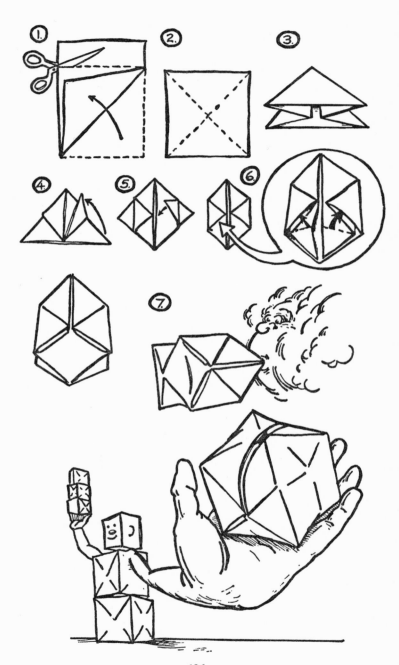

106

Now lift one of the bottom points of the triangle and fold it upward toward the top of the triangle, as shown on the right-hand side of figure 4. Do the same with the opposite point; when finished, it will resemble the left-hand side of figure 4.

Turn the paper over and do the same with the lower points of the triangle on the other side. You now have a square on end, the same shape and orientation as a baseball diamond. Take the points at left and right—first and third base—and fold to the center (figure 5). Turn over and do the same on the other side, to attain the shape shown in the small drawing in figure 6.

Now comes the tricky part. There are a pair of little loose triangular flaps at the bottom of the developing water-bomb. Lift them, crease them across the middle, away from you, and insert into the spaces shown in the flaps above them, as the detail drawing in figure 6 illustrates. Turn over and do the same on the other side.

You now have figure 7. The water-bomb is finished, and needs only to be inflated to be ready for use. Of course, you may store the collapsed units in any convenient space until ready. It remains only to blow briskly through the open end of the bomb to inflate it. Then fill it up with water and wait for a passerby, or just tug at the corners with your fingers until it snaps into a perfect cube. Pile them up as high as you like, then invite the neighbors in.

STEPPING THROUGH
A SMALL PIECE OF PAPER

Let's say you're sitting in your office, classroom, or living room, totally fed up with what's going on around you, which is probably nothing at all. You pick up a small piece of paper, no more than six inches square, and say to the person next to you, "Hey, I bet you $100,000 I can step right through this small piece of paper, even pull it over my entire body, all the way over my head." Very cute, they say, then dare you. So you do. They stare. They gape. They burst into extended applause. Maybe, even, they lose a small bet. Here's how:

The piece of paper should be as small as possible—but no less than six inches per side. Nonchalantly fold the paper in half (figures 1 and 2).

With a scissors, or tearing with your fingers, make a slit every half-inch or so. Alternate the slits so that one starts on the folded side, the next on the open side (figure 3).

After you've made your slits, cut or tear along the folded side, making sure you do not cut or tear the fold at the top or bottom of the paper (see figure 3).

When you're all finished, look your victim right in the

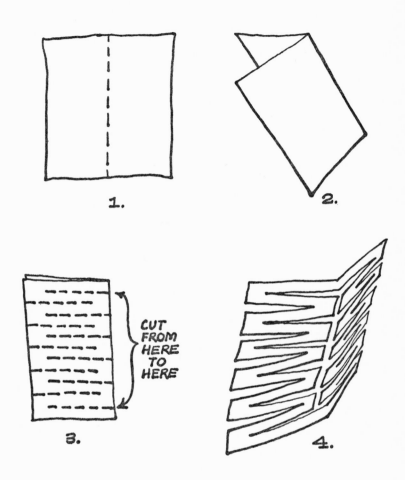

eye, then unfold your little piece of paper. It will open up into an enormous, glorious ring (figure 4).

Now put the ring down on the floor, step inside, and pull it up over your body, then over your noggin. Collect your winnings with a smile and, when the chump asks what you do for an encore, play dumb (and deaf).

THE POOR MAN'S
INSTANT CAMERA

This construction combines the customary ingenuity and manual dexterity that all show-offs have so much of, with elements of the put-on, together with a dash of fashionable modern financial planning. Here's what happens: suppose your friends are talking about the high price of everything today. You interrupt, saying that you've found a way to beat at least the high cost of photography; you've found an instant camera that costs a lot less than a dollar. Of course, nobody will believe this, so you've got to prove it.

You pull out of your pocket, not a camera, but a piece of paper with a drawing of a camera on it. No one is impressed by that, so you say you're going to use the camera to take a friend's portrait. You hold up the "camera" in front of someone's face and ask him to watch the birdie. You give a quick snap to the paper and ZIP! where the "camera" was is now a cartoon face—his "portrait." If this makes your friend so angry he tears up the camera and stomps on it, that's all right, because you can make another one in a few minutes. Here's how:

1. Take a piece of paper about twice as long as it is wide—say 6 by 12 inches—and fold it across the middle, into two identical more-or-less-square halves.

2. Decide where the corners of the "camera" are going to be, and punch four holes with a sharp pencil through both halves of the folded paper. If you don't like the marks the pencil leaves, use a pin; just be sure that the holes are identically located on both halves of the folded paper.

3. Unfold the paper and lay it flat, with the side that was inside the fold down. With a sharp knife or scissors, cut vertical slits between the top and bottom holes on each half of the paper, as shown in figure 3; then cut a horizontal slit between the lower pair of holes on each half of the paper. You now have a loose flap on each half of the paper, with the loose edge at the bottom. On the lower half of the paper, draw a funny face, keeping it all inside the edges of the flap. Outside the flap, draw the body of the camera and add a tripod, a squeeze-bulb and, if you like, a birdie for authenticity. When you're finished with this step, the paper should resemble figure 3.

4. Turn the paper over, being sure to turn it left-to-right, not end-for-end. Inside the top flap, draw the lens and bellows of the camera as shown in figure 4.

5. Fold the paper back the way it was in step 2. The funny face is now exposed on the front of the "camera." To load the camera, open up the paper a little and tuck the "lens" forward, while you tuck the funny face backwards. The bellows and lens overlap the funny face through the hole in the paper, and now appear on the front of the camera as in figure 5. The camera is now loaded and ready to take a comic picture of anyone.

Now, to shoot the camera, just open and shut the folded paper about halfway in a quick, snappy motion. The lens disappears and funny face jumps into view. Go find your best friend and photograph him before the film goes stale. It's true this instant camera has limitations—everybody tends to look alike and, even worse, everybody looks even uglier than usual.

WORLD'S GREATEST
CAT'S CRADLE

Once upon a time, everybody knew how to make elaborate cat's cradles. Like a lot of other manual skills, this too is passing, which is bad for America but good for the show-off. The less everybody else knows, the more brightly does the knowledge of the show-off shine.

Not only are cat's cradles very pretty, they require only a piece of string and two idle hands, articles very easy to come by these days. The next time you see a piece of string being used for some sensible purpose, like package wrapping, interrupt the whole activity by seizing the string, and become the center of attention by producing this magnificent cat's cradle.

Look at figure 9 to see what you're going to get. Splendid, yes? All right, here's how to get it. Follow these instructions carefully, and be sure at all times that you're handling only the strings we tell you to; otherwise, horrible confusion will crop up. Ready?

Take a piece of string not less than six feet long, preferably seven, and tie it into a loop. Pick up the loop with both hands, as shown in figure 1 (all illustrations are drawn from your own point of view), with the string crossing the palms between finger and thumb.

With your right index finger, reach over to your left palm and pick up the string on the back of the finger (figure 2). Pull the string taut by separating your hands. Now do the exact reverse action with your left hand, resulting in figure 3. You now have a loop of string over each index finger.

Without disturbing the other strings, reach over with your right hand, pick the loop off your left index finger, and drop it over your left wrist. Pull taut, do the exact reverse action with the left hand working on the right, and pull taut again. Now things have reached the state shown in figure 4.

You now have a loop over each pinky, each thumb, and each wrist. With the right hand, grab the string just in front of the left pinky, pull out a little slack, draw the string across the left palm, and drop it over the left thumb, creating a new loop over the thumb. Then, with the right hand, grab the string that was already there on the left thumb—not the one you just put there—grasping it on the opposite side of the thumb from your face, pull out some slack, and drop it over the left pinky (refer to the left hand of figure 5 to see how the strings ought to go). Now repeat exactly, using the left hand to work on the right-hand strings. You should now have figure 5.

Now, see where all those strings come together in the middle of figure 5? Seize the whole bunch right in the middle with your left hand and lay them over the crotch of your right thumb onto the back of your right hand (figure 6). You will see that there are two loops of string around your right thumb; carefully grab both loops with your left hand, pull them straight up off the right thumb, and keep hold of them while allowing the whole mess of string on the back of your right hand to pass upward and clear of your right thumb (figure 7). Then, with your left hand, put the two loops you're holding back on your right

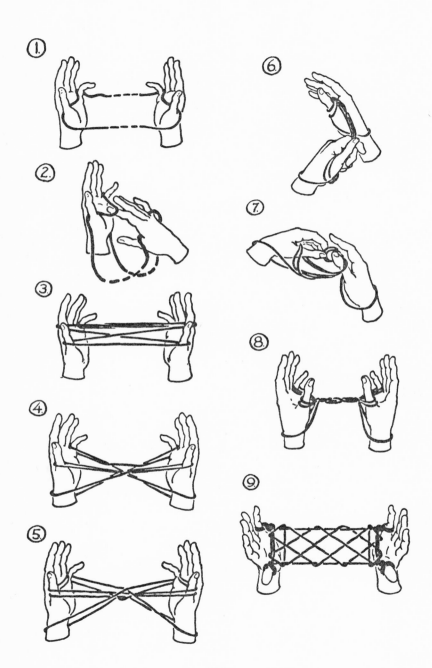

117

thumb, just the way they were. Now do the same thing exactly, using your right hand, to the strings on your left hand. You have now attained figure 8.

Using your right hand, reach over your left hand, pick up the loop around your left wrist, pull it up and over your left hand, let go, dropping the string into the middle between your hands. Do the same thing with your left hand to the loop of string around your right wrist.

Now the amazing part happens. Draw the string taut by separating your hands and there you are: figure 9! That's if you've been very careful to follow the instructions and not dropped any strings. If you don't have figure 9, go back and start over, because it's in the string waiting for you to find it.

THE ART OF
SELF-UGLIFICATION

It seems probable that primitive man's first show-off trick was to make a nasty face. Primitive man just stuck out his tongue and crossed his eyes; civilization taught him to draw out the corners of his mouth with his pinky fingers while shoving his nose upward with his thumbs. Nowadays, technology and imagination allow the use of artificial aids in face-making. With the three simple devices we're about to show you, you'll be able to make a face so nasty your mother will rue the day you were taught to read. Here goes, in three easy steps.

1. Walnut Monster Eyes:

Obtain a large English walnut and carefully divide it into two perfect halves. Eat the meat, and clean out the inside of each half of the shell with sandpaper until there are no rough edges. Then take a twist drill of one-eighth inch diameter or smaller and bore a hole dead in the middle of each shell (figure 1). Put the shells in your eyes, monocle fashion, crinkling the cheeks slightly if necessary to hold them in place. You should be able to see out pretty well. Now look in a mirror. Revolting!

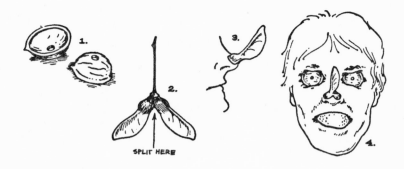

SPLIT HERE

2. Green Nose Thing:

Get a fresh green maple seed (of course you have to wait until they are falling from the trees in your neighborhood). Maple seeds are the kind that look like figure 2.

Break off one half of the maple seed and throw it away. Take the other and, using a sharp fingernail or a paring knife, split the seed end, leaving the flying-wing end intact. As long as the seed was fresh and green to start with, the inside of the seed will be all sticky—sticky enough that you can make it adhere to the end of your nose, sticking up in the air like the proboscis of some horrible bug (figure 3).

3. Orange Monolith Teeth:

Peel an orange, taking care to keep the peel in large pieces. Find a piece of the peel that's the right size to insert between your lips but in front of your teeth, so when you smile all that appears is a hideous orange grin. Some people use lemons, but on the whole the effect of orange peel is more interesting.

Now that you've practiced all the parts, put them together (figure 4). Now go out on the street, and see how long it takes before dogs begin to bark and you hear that distant siren wail that means you're striking terror throughout the city!

Part Four:
So You Want To Be
A Stuntman

A DRUGSTORE COWBOY
LASSOS AN ICE CUBE

This little number combines the show-off properties of ice cubes with the show-off properties of string—both articles easy to find, but not usually found in the same place at the same time, except in old-fashioned general stores with soda fountains. In order to score prestige points by lassoing an ice cube, it's usually necessary to carry the string with you down to the drugstore counter and order the glass of water separately. The string should be the cotton kind, fibrous and easy to soak with water— positively not the new-fangled nylon or synthetic sort that hardly gets wet at all.

So, here's what you do. You tie a one-or-two-inch loop in the end of the piece of string, sit down at the counter, and ask for a glass of ice water. The ice has to be in cubes, of course. Then you ask your nearest neighbor if he thinks he can remove the ice cube from the water by using the loop of string. He is not allowed to touch the glass with his fingers, or indeed to move the glass in any way. If you've picked a sensible victim, his most probable response will be: "No, I can't, and you can't either." Your only way out

of this dilemma is to insist in a firm voice that you can so. Try to sound positive. Make him believe it. Then let him try (figure 1).

After he's tried and failed long enough, then you step in. Your secret, of course, is that you cheat. You simply lower the loop onto the exposed top surface of the floating ice cube, so it just lies there on top of the cube. Try to get it to lie as flat as you can. Then, take a pinch of salt and sprinkle it on top of the ice cube, string and all (figure 2). Wait a few seconds. The action of the salt on the ice cube will freeze the string solid to the cube. Then all you have to do is pick it up (figure 3). Astounding! Of course, you probably won't want to drink the water after this. If your victim objects that you didn't say you were going to use salt in this trick, the best answer is that you didn't say you weren't.

This can also be done with a toothpick—the flat kind, not the round torpedo-shaped product—by simply adding water to the glass until the top of the ice cube is level with the top of the glass. The toothpick is then rested on the rim of the glass and the ice cube, and the end of it that's on the cube is salted. Seconds later, you can pick up the cube using the toothpick as a handle. It works just as well this way, but the string method is more spectacular, and the show-off, given any kind of choice, always prefers the flashy by a wide margin.

HOW TO BE A
TWENTY-CARD WIZARD

Everybody knows some kind of card trick; the difference between a show-off's superior card trick and an ordinary citizen's hum-drum everyday card trick lies, in this case, in sheer magnitude. Allowing one person to pick a card, and then correctly identifying it, is impressive; two is better; three is astonishing; but today's mastermind manipulation permits the show-off to allow up to ten people to pick cards, and then spot them all correctly. It boggles—think of the glory!—ten minds at once. Of course, if you can't find ten willing participants, it works just as well with fewer, down to and including one.

The effect is this: You shuffle a deck of cards (or let anyone else shuffle it) as much as you like and then deal ten pairs face down—a total of twenty cards in stacks of two. You turn your back or leave the room or offer to be blindfolded while your victims choose pairs, pick them up, examine them, memorize them, and put them back down— in any order at all, provided the pairs stay together. You re-enter the room, pick up all the pairs, and lay them out face up in four rows of five cards each. You ask any

participant in the stunt to tell you which of the four rows
his cards are in. If he tells the truth, you are able instantly
to pick up the two cards he selected, and hand them to
him. He retires in awe and embarrassment, and you proceed to do the same with as many participants as are on
hand. Of course, if you're showing off to the full ten
players, there will be only two cards left when you get to
number ten, so he may not be as astonished as number
one. O.K., here's how you do it:

To be a twenty-card wizard, you must memorize the
following chart of four magic words:

ATLAS
BIBLE
THIGH
GOOSE

Notice that there are ten letters used in these four
words, that each letter is used only twice, and that each

word contains one and only one pair of letters: two A's in ATLAS, and so on. This should give you a clue as to how the trick actually works. The best way to learn the chart is to practice by getting a big sheet of paper and drawing the chart full-size—large enough to lay one card on top of each letter.

Now, clear the table and begin to practice. Deal ten pairs of cards face down. Impersonate a spectator by looking at one pair and memorizing it. Now pick up all the pairs into a stack, turn it face up, and lay out the cards face up on the chart like this: put the first card you come to on one of the A's in ATLAS: the second card, on the other A. The next card goes on one of the T's; the next, on the other T. The next two cards are placed on the L's; the next two, on the S's; and so on. This will be a slow, awkward process at first. Do not lose heart. Your object is to learn to do it quickly, gracefully, and finally, without using an actual chart but working from your memory.

Now, when you have all the cards laid out, look for the two you picked. Whatever they were, they'll be on top of a pair of letters. If, say, they are in the first and fourth rows, they have to be the cards on S. If they are both in the second row, they have to be the cards on B; and so on.

When you have the chart thoroughly memorized, go forth and seek a roomful of suckers. Deal the pairs, and let your victims select one card pair each; lay out the cards according to the magic words ATLAS, BIBLE, THIGH, GOOSE. Do not, of course, be so careless as to whisper the words aloud, but store them safely in your memory. Ask the players to show you which row their cards are in. Unerringly you pick the right ones, thereby making up to ten people wish they, too, could be show-offs in the same class as yourself.

THE CALCULATED
SHOW-OFF

All a person really needs to show off is a wonderfully warped sense of him/herself. Very rarely is extra equipment necessary. This time, though, we'll tell you how to get some mileage out of those new fangled pocket calculators that you see advertised on TV.

Take a pocket calculator and hand it to a friend or a sucker. Tell him to enter the number 8777 and multiply it by four. Ask him what he's got. When he tells you, tell him he's wrong. Tell him he's got the capital of Idaho. When he tells you you're nuts, take the calculator and turn it upside down. There, spelled out in what may easily pass for letters of the alphabet, B O I S E. Get it?

Most numbers on the calculator, when looked at upside down, resemble letters of the alphabet, like this:

1 2 3 4 5 7 8 9 0
I Z E h S L B G O

You may not believe this if you don't have a calculator in front of you; when you do, however, you'll see what we mean.

What other unbelievable stunts can you do with the

calculator? Tell another chump that your calculator can actually bring an oil company to his house. Tell him to enter the number 710.77345. When he looks at you funny, turn the machine over and show him what's what (as in the drawing here). He may think you're crazy but at least he'll respect you. Other calculating ideas to try: 0.7734 equals HELLO: 4509 equals GOSH; 2572 plus 87 times 12 equals the nickname of the male lead in "Casablanca."

Finally, one more trick. Ask your chump to enter his age on the calculator, then double it. Now, add 5 and multiply by 50. Tell him to add the amount of change in his pocket, up to a dollar. Now, subtract the number of days in a year, add 115, divide by 100. Your result will be his age, then a decimal, then the amount of change in his pocket. We've checked it and it works. If you try and it doesn't, don't blame us.

A RIDICULOUS
TEST OF STRENGTH

All show-offs are outer-directed people. It's impossible to show off without an audience. Nothing, therefore, gives us greater pleasure than to tell you about a fellow show-off, Dominic Valentine. Dominic lives in Philadelphia, where he employs the following stunt to win bets in bars. We don't recommend it to everybody, since, as you shall see, there is an element of risk involved, not to mention an element of looking awfully dumb if you fail. Later on we'll give you a foolproof method of showing your strength. But first, here's how Dominic proves that he's the strongest man in any bar in Philadelphia:

1. He obtains a willing subject (hopefully one who's not awfully big), gets him to lie down on the floor, and has him tighten his belt as snug as possible, with the excess belt sticking straight out in front.

2. He then leans over the subject's middle, placing both hands, palms down, just above the knees, as in football set position. He instructs the subject to fold his arms across his chest and to hold his body rigid, no matter what. Having checked to see that the belt is strong, and without

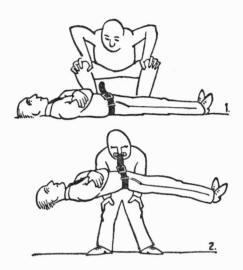

a lot of stretch in it, he takes a comfortable amount of the subject's belt between his teeth.

3. He then clamps down on the belt and begins to rise.

We haven't met Dominic Valentine personally—he wrote us a letter about all this—but, to tell the truth, we're scared of him.

If you haven't got what it takes to pull people off the floor with your teeth—or don't especially want to find out if you do—here's a deceitful test of strength you'll always win:

1. Place your fingertips together in front of your chest.

2. Challenge the strongest man around to seize your arms just above the elbows and pull your fingers apart. No jerking, just steady pressure, applied any way he wants to (use of feet not allowed). Unless you're too puny to be reading this book, the mechanical set-up is such that you'll be able to resist anybody short of King Kong.

THE ENCHANTED BOAT

Three-fourths of the surface of the earth is water, so there's no telling where the show-off may run into a glass of the stuff. If you drink it, well and good. But when you've had enough, you're sure to begin playing with it, using it to impress your friends and vex your enemies. This little jape is almost self-explanatory, once we've explained it, but the solution is not likely to occur out of a blue sky. You might even use it to win a bet or two; we'll leave the set-up and the patter to you, but here's the elementary physics of the thing:

Start with a glass of water, almost full to the top (but not quite) and hand it, with a sort of cockeyed smile, to the audience of your choice (figure 1).

Fashion a tiny boat of any available material. Actually it doesn't have to be a boat, just something that will float high on the water, but in practice what works best is a boat-shaped object bent out of a little bit of tin foil, like figure 2.

Drop the boat on the surface of the water and challenge all comers to make it stay in the middle of the glass.

Don't worry. No matter how hard anyone tries, or how often they push it to the middle, it will always float off-center and adhere to the side of the glass (figure 3). Why? Because of the surface tension of the water is why; the phenomenon known as capillarity, which you can look up in the encyclopedia, forces it to the side every time. Now, place your bet that you and you alone can make the boat stay in the middle.

All right, the pay-off. Fill up the glass above the rim (figure 4). If your muscles are steady enough to do this free-hand, well and good; if you have trouble, do it by filling the glass as high as you can and then gently dropping pennies or something in. You'll be surprised how high you can stack the water in a bulge on top of the glass. The boat, to everyone's great satisfaction, now moves to the center of the glass and stays there.

Now that you've won, prove what a good sport you are by ordering a round of water for the whole table!

HOW TO PUSH A PENCIL
WITH YOUR MIND

A strong mind can do just about anything, though it can't move a mountain. It can, however, move a pencil across a table, and that's a fact. With the help of our brilliant assistant shown here, we will teach you how to move a pencil across a surface, without ever touching it.

In figure 1, our assistant holds up an ordinary pencil. For purposes that will remain a secret, make sure you use a round pencil, not one with edges.

In figure 2, our assistant begins summoning his strong mind to action. This is achieved by shaking the hands and arms. This action activates the very complicated "force-fields" that will ultimately move the pencil.

In figure 3 our assistant begins to circle the pencil with his finger. This action defines the "force-field" further and serves to focus all mental attention on the object. Make slow circles at first; then make a number of frenzied circles while increasing your mental concentration.

In figure 4, our assistant is shown making the pencil roll away from him. He is not, as you can see, touching the pencil with his hands. No, the pencil is miraculously fol-

1.

2.

3.

4.

lowing the man's finger, no strings attached. Well, one sort of string: our assistant is gently blowing air on the table's surface behind the pencil. He does this quietly and without notice.

The wild hand movements, you see, have distracted the audience's attention. So it looks as though nothing whatsoever is making the pencil move—nothing except the summoning of mental powers and a lot of ridiculous arm waving and finger circles. Practice by yourself—then go find someone to astound.

In the event your mind is not strong enough to move a pencil, forget about the pencil and use a cigarette. Cigarettes are a lot lighter than pencils; don't strain your mind unnecessarily

TAKING OFF YOUR VEST WITHOUT TAKING OFF YOUR COAT

A show-off is truthful, and to tell the truth, fellow show-offs, we don't feel like giving you the hard sell on this one. Oh, we could invent scenarios, pointing out terrific opportunities for self- display, invoking hordes of admiring beauties, jealous athletes and envious international spies. But if you don't immediately see the tremendous opportunities in knowing how to take off your vest without taking off your coat, you're simply not the show-off we took you for.

Here's how it's done. Unbutton your jacket and your vest (if you hoped we'd show you how to do it with both buttoned, we're sorry, because that's impossible). All right, now reach down and grab the left-hand corner of your jacket and stuff it into the left armhole of your vest (figure 1).

Keep on stuffing the material of your coat into your vest through the left armhole until you can't manage any more. Only then slip your left arm and shoulder—fully clothed with your jacket—out of the vest—(figure 2). This will be a little bit awkward, but not impossible. Just go

easy and don't tear anything; if it doesn't seem to be working, calm down and fuss with it until things go smoothly.

Once you've got your left arm free, reach around behind and pull more of your coat through that left armhole of the vest. As the coat passes through the vest, the vest passes across your back toward your right shoulder. When you've gone about as far as you can go, bring your right shoulder and arm (and the jacket that's on them both) through the armhole of the vest (figure 3). Once again, take it easy. If you find yourself totally confused, take the whole thing off and start again. If you've done everything right, you are now wearing the vest on your right shoulder only, sort of flopping down your side under the jacket.

Finally, using your left hand, grab some loose vest near the shoulder and stuff it into your right coat sleeve from the inside. Keep pushing your vest into your right sleeve until you can reach some of the vest from the other end of the sleeve—the hand end, that is. When that's possible, just reach into the sleeve from the outside, grab the vest, and pull it out through the sleeve (figure 4).

Now, if you've done it right, your coat is still one hundred percent on, and your vest is one hundred percent off. If you want to learn this the easy way, find a friend who will stand still while you do it to him; after you see from the outside exactly how it works, you'll find it easier to do to yourself. Of course, your clothes get a little rumpled up this way and may need to be pressed afterwards, but we never promised you a thornless rose garden, did we?

HOW TO RECEIVE
BRAIN MESSAGES

This book can show you lots of ways to exploit the real world for your personal glory. This feat will show you how to exploit the unreal world. The dandy psychic experiment below will mystify your most cynical acquaintances. All you need is a telephone directory, a pencil, a piece of paper. And, of course, your own finely tuned extra-sensory-perception (heh, heh). But before you go any further, get out the phone book and turn to page 89. Memorize the tenth name from the top of the far-right column on that page. Now go find your subject.

Tell your subject to write down any three digits, no two of which can be the same. Now tell him to reverse the order of these numbers. In figure one, the subject has chosen 742 (which in reverse is 247). Now tell the subject to subtract the smaller figure from the larger.

Ask the subject if he is left with three digits. If he is, move on to the next step. If he has only two digits, tell him to put a zero in front of them.

Tell your subject to take the result of what he has just subtracted and reverse the numbers. In figure two, for

instance, 495 is reversed to 594. Tell your subject to add these together. The sum is 1089.

The sum is *always* 1089, no matter what three numbers were picked at the outset. And that's how this all works. Ask the subject to turn to the page in the phone book designed by his last two numbers (89). Tell him to count down from the top the number of names designated by the first two digits (10). Tell him to concentrate on this name.

You make a big deal about trying to receive his brain waves. Then tell him what the first name is—now the last. You've had it memorized all along, remember? Your subject will fall down dead!

BLOWING SMOKE RINGS

This peaceful, quiet classic is useful for a small group of intimate friends, or just one friend, if that's all you have. It conveys the impression of thoughtfulness; whenever you blow smoke rings you look as though you were thinking of something else—maybe something important (lots of luck).

It is useful to know that pipe or cigar smoke works better than cigarette smoke, though cigarette smoke will do if there are no drafts in the room. It's not necessary to inhale in order to blow wonderful rings; it's better all around, in fact, if you don't. Inhaled smoke is less dense than non-inhaled smoke and doesn't hang together as well when pushed out of the mouth toward the ceiling. To blow smoke rings, light up and then follow these steps:

1. Draw in enough smoke to fill your mouth. Try to keep it toward the back of your mouth so it won't escape until you want it to.

2. Purse your lips into a tiny, perfectly round O. Rest your tongue lightly on the floor of your mouth. Keep all muscles relaxed.

3. Without changing the shape of the O, increase its size by pulling your upper lip tightly against your upper teeth and dropping your lower jaw slightly. The O at this stage should be about an inch in diameter.

4. Push out the ring by gently flicking your tongue. The back of the tongue is what does the trick; at no time should you stick your tongue out of your mouth. Each mouthful of smoke yields four or five puffy smoke rings. Pause briefly between rings so that one air-current doesn't interfere with the next.

YOUR BASIC
JEW'S HARP INSTRUCTION

Once upon a time, before the transistor radio, just about every kid in America had a Jew's harp (so called for being a leading article of peddler's merchandise in the nineteenth century, but now sometimes sold as the Mouth Harp). Today you can show off with a Jew's harp merely by owning one, for very few people under forty even know what one looks like.

The Jew's harp is a simple lyre-shaped piece of steel with a vibrating reed between its two ends (see figure 1). It is extremely useful for showing off at parties because it can be easily carried in a shirt pocket, because it's easy to play, and because you can just about count on nobody else having one. Yet they are available at any big music store. A word of caution: don't buy a small, cheap, tinny instrument. The big ones are cheap enough, goodness knows, and work a lot better. Now, here's how to play it:

Hold the big end in your left hand and place the two legs flat against your teeth. The hooked end of the reed should point away from your face. Now open your mouth wide enough so the reed, which you're going to pluck in a

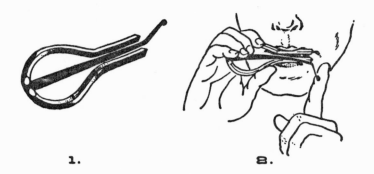

1.   **2.**

minute, can pass between your teeth on the backswing. Close your lips on the instrument just enough to hold it in place firmly against your teeth without a lot of pressure from the left hand (figure 2).

Ready? Pluck the end of the reed with your right index finger. If you're doing everything right, you should hear a rich harmonious twang. If you fail to hear music at this point you may be doing something wrong like:

1. Biting the instrument. This presses the legs together so the reed hits them with a clank.

2. Not opening your teeth wide enough. If the reed actually strikes your teeth, you get an ugly whacking rattle that hurts.

3. Not maintaining firm contact between your teeth and the body of the instrument. If you just hold it with your lips the sound is dull and muffled, because the vibrations aren't passing through your teeth into the echo-chambers of your skull. On the other hand, don't press so hard that you do nasty things to your teeth; a show-off doesn't need dental problems.

O.K., so now you have a tone but not a tune. To control the pitch, close off the bottom of your throat (this can be accomplished by consciously breathing through your nose). Now, while plucking rhythmically on the reed, move your tongue up and down in your mouth exactly as though you were humming or whistling or singing. See?

154

The pitch changes. It takes only a few minutes' practice to get reasonable control of the intonation; perfect pitch may require a little longer.

Anything you can whistle, you can play on the Jew's harp. The conventional way to strum is in a rapid rhythm, treating everything like a banjo tune, plinky-plink, plinky-plink, but you can slow down for ballads and spirituals. "Boing-boing" effects are particularly easy and satisfying. And for a rich (but tonally uncontrollable) bass pedal-point, open your throat and let the whole column of air right down to your lungs resonate. From here on out, you'll be the life of every party. You could be almost as much fun with a banjo, but people would be able to see you and your banjo-case coming a mile away; with a handy pocket-size Jew's harp, noboby knows you're about to start showing off until it's toq late.

WHAT MAKES
SAMMY HUSTLE?

If there's a pool table in your basement, or if you're old and brave enough to make an occasional stop down at your town's billiard emporium, what follows will be of great help to you.

There are two ways to show off at pool. The first is to be able to actually *play* pool, to run a string of fifty balls while your opponent stands there with his teeth in his mouth. The second way is to possess a bit of wit and a touch of sneak. Well, nice to meet you. Here are a couple of neat feats you can pull when it's your opponent who gets hot and you're the one standing there with your teeth in your mouth.

Our first maneuver is sinking a wine glass in an end pocket. This should be practiced in private before it is attempted for an audience. Any wine glass will do so long as it curves on the table when rolled. A glass that rolls in a straight line is no good. Once you've made a number of attempts, you'll be able to place the glass at exactly the right spot. Figure 1 shows an example of one glass's rolling habits.

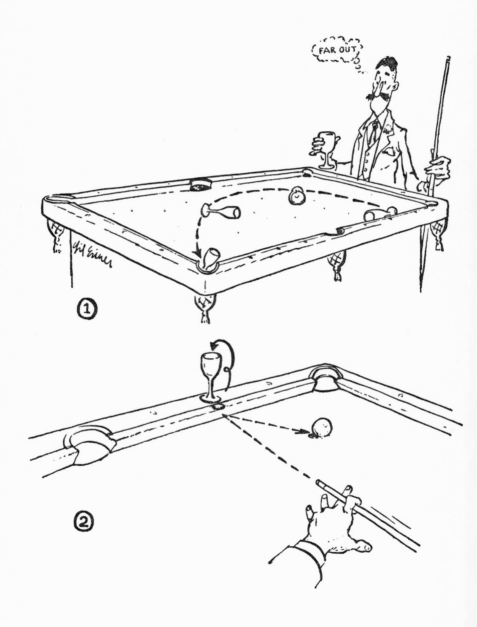

158

In practice, the glass should be placed at the mouth of the pocket and pushed with your finger *away* from the pocket. The spot at which it consistently stops is the spot you should start from when actually performing.

Once you have a glass that can be trusted, stick with it. One thing to remember: when pushing the glass with your finger, always push firmly. A glass pushed by a finger that slips off the edge of the glass will go awry.

Our second hustle is this. Tell your victim you can hit a ball with your cue, strike a coin on the table, then drive that coin into an upright glass. You can use the same glass as in the trick above. To do this, place the glass on the table's edge, as shown in figure 2, and put your coin on the edge of the table, just in front of the glass. Now strike a ball from across the table in a direct line toward the coin and glass. Some practice shots will tell you how strong to hit. Correctly performed, the coin will pop up and fall into the glass with a triumphant ping.

A NEW TRICK
FOR AN OLD BOTTLE

The difficult the show-off does immediately; the impossible, even faster than that. This impossible stunt requires, by way of materials, an empty soda or beer bottle (or any other kind of bottle with a small top, small enough that a quarter won't fall through), a newspaper, and a pocketful of change.

Assuming you have these things, just look around for someone who doesn't sufficiently respect your powers. When you find him, ask him to watch while you cut (or tear; scissors are helpful but not absolutely necessary) a strip about a foot long and an inch wide from the newspaper. Lay it across the bottle top. Then stack some odd change—say a quarter, a nickel, a dime and maybe a penny—on top of the paper strip and the bottle top. Ready? Now dare your victim to remove the paper and leave the coins in place. He is not allowed to touch the bottle or the coins, or permit or cause them to be touched by anything. Doesn't look so awfully hard, does it? Let him try. No matter how gently he tugs and jiggles at the paper, the coins will inevitably cascade off in a jingle of

failed hopes. He may try pulling the paper out in one
grand jerk; same result. He may light the paper with a
match, hoping to burn it out; but the best he'll get is a
circle of scorched paper, still firmly in place under the
coins.

All right, now it's your turn. Exhibit your superiority
in the following manner: without touching either the
bottle or the coins, cut or tear one end of the paper right
across, as close to the bottle-top as possible (see the dotted
line in the drawing? closer than that, even, if you can).

Your victim may object at this point: "You didn't say
I could cut the paper." The correct reply to that is: "I
didn't say you couldn't." Look smug as you answer.

Then, grasp the other end of the paper—the one you
didn't cut off—and hit the paper strip a sharp whack with
your free hand, or the side of the scissors, or something,
midway between the end you're holding and the bottle

top. Zip! out comes the paper, leaving the coins and bottle exactly as they were. How come? Because the inertia of the coins is sufficient to resist the friction of the paper for the split second necessary to get the paper out of there. You now have the paper in one hand, and the coins resting firmly on the bottle. You have conquered. Open another bottle and enjoy the glory that is yours.

More Sneaky Feats

TO SARAH FERRELL AND VANESSA JALET

for tolerating all this

NOT AN INTRODUCTION

As the title of this book indicates, there was another one like it before. In the Introduction to that one *(Sneaky Feats: The Art of Showing Off and 53 Ways to Do It)* numerous historical parallels were adduced—from Cain and Abel through Daniel Boone, George Washington, Babe Ruth and Bobby Riggs—to demonstrate, illustrate, explicate and justify the role of the show-off in all stages of society hitherto discovered—especially now, and especially in America. The inference is clear: there is no real reason for another Introduction like that one.

Setting aside, therefore, the question of an Introduction, there remains the larger question of why there should even be a second and successor volume to the first. For one thing, this present book is published in recognition of the unanimously generous reception accorded to its predecessor. One reviewer, writing in the *Yale Daily News Magazine*, went so far as to say something like (we lost the actual clipping): "If you had the money to buy this book, you could probably buy something worse with it." No one has laid a glove on us yet—what more could we have asked?

Clearly, our message is getting through. To show off—to search for glory and recognition by learning to do things nobody else can do, and then finding ways to compel everybody else to watch you do them—is the vital element itself, the very stuff of which life is made. Look about you: all over the literate world, unprecedented feats of goldfish-swallowing and endurance-unicycle-riding are being conceived and executed for no other reason than to get their performers included in *The Guinness Book of World Records*. In every nation, literate or not, men and women strain every nerve and muscle preparing for the next Olympic Games, all of them hoping to run, swim, jump, or throw some kind of object faster, higher, or farther than ever before—and on television, if possible. Closer to home, hundreds of men and women in ridiculous costumes are lined up at this very moment in the effort to attract attention on "Let's Make A Deal." And as we write these words, the United States itself is engaged in a vast propaganda effort, sparing no technique of publicity or self-promotion, to make the world take heed that 1976 is its two-hundredth birthday. No one there is that doesn't love a show-off, or doesn't want to be one. It is in our blood.

Therefore this book. Once is never enough; if it were, there would be only one tower in the World Trade Center, instead of two; only one pyramid at Gizeh, instead of three; only one face carved out of Mount Rushmore, instead of four, or is it five?

The techniques of showing off that follow have been divided into significant sections, each calculated to teach you skills that will command, however unwillingly, the admiration and envy of spectators. The first of these, "Tricks For All Trades," provides an assortment of offhand stunts, using simple props, that will make people fear and respect your name, whatever it is (and remember it, too). "Cheap Thrills With Real Money" shows you a number of ways, none costing more than a dollar, to raise rapid interest in your immediate vicinity. "Knot So Fast, Buster!" is a short course in manual dexterity with knots, strings, silk scarves, and whatnot, that will bind other people's attention inseparably to you. "The Power to Cloud Men's Minds" is a handy compendium of brain tricks, calculated to drive the audience of your choice stark bonkers. Finally, "Looky What You Made!" exhibits the show-off in his role as creator, making all manner of things to amaze and confound innocent bystanders, who probably wanted to be left alone, thank you.

—Tom Ferrell
Lee Eisenberg
New York
January 1, 1976

Part Five:
Tricks For All Trades

TEARING A PHONE BOOK
IN HALF

Here it is, fellow show-offs, the greatest strong-man stunt in history, all yours. And all you have to know in order to perform this trick is how to cheat. You're going to want to wait until summer before trying this one, because, as you'll see, you're going to want the windows open. You're also going to want to live in or near a big city where you can get some big-city phone books, because almost anybody can tear the Medicine Bow phone book in two without cheating.

To prepare, collect some dandy big phone books—the 1,700-page Manhattan is the classic. You're going to need some to practice on and some for performances.

Go into the kitchen, open all the windows, turn on all the fans, and set the oven at 350 degrees—no hotter, because you don't want the phone book to catch fire. Put the phone book in the oven and wait. How long you'll have to wait depends on how old and brittle your phone book is to begin with.

You must have all the windows open because baking phone books are smelly. It's not a repulsive rotten-egg killer smell, it's more like a fire in the basement. It will make you cough and your eyes will hurt, unless you keep the place well ventilated.

After about three hours, take the phone book out of the oven, using kitchen hot-pads so you don't get burned. This is a hot phone book now. Gingerly lift the cover and fold back the corner of a page to see if it's getting brittle. If it tends to crumble in your fingers, that's enough; if not, put it back in the oven until it is done.

When the phone book is done, put it in the back yard or out on the fire escape to cool. This will take a couple of hours all by itself, and by now the smell should have cleared out.

1.

2.

Ready? Pick up the phone book with the binding toward you. Hold the book as shown in figure 1, bending it slightly to bevel the pages so you start tearing one page at a time instead of the whole thing at once. Take a firm grip and give an enormous, slow, massive tug. Rrrrrrip! (figure 2).

If the phone book fails to go rrrrrip, that's because you didn't cook it long enough. Remember that for your next effort.

When you have a supply of nicely baked phone books, just leave them around the house until some day when the neighbors are over. They say, casually, "Betcha I can tear a New York (or Los Angeles, or Chicago) phone book in two."

Then, like the winner that you are, *Do it!*

A BELT WHERE IT HURTS

You know how it drives you nuts when you're trying to learn something new—something new and not really worth doing, like long division or taking square roots—and you can't seem really to get the hang of it and it drives you wild with fury? Well, this is your opportunity to turn the tables on the world, with a stunt you can perform over and over on some hapless victim who should know better by now than to mess with an accomplished show-off. Fortunately for you, hapless victims never learn.

Here's what you do: you take off your belt (or bring an extra one along), double it in the middle, roll it up tight, and put it on a table. You invite an onlooker to stick a pencil (or a butcher knife, or a gilded dagger, or anything) into the center of the belt, so that when you try to snatch it away he will catch it by the loop in the middle. What could seem easier? Well, nothing is easier, as a matter of fact, since the first time he tries it he succeeds. Then you make your move: you bet him that he'll never succeed again. And as long as you follow these instructions carefully, he never will. You can snatch the belt away from the pencil again and again—he'll never find the middle in a million tries.

All right, here's how. Study carefully the drawing of the rolled-up belt. Remember, you double it in the middle first, then you roll it up in a tight coil toward the ends. Please note (this is important): the belt should be doubled before rolling so the tongue end will be on the outside of the coil, and a little shorter than the buckle end. Take off your belt and try it, you'll get the idea.

Now, every belt (anyhow, most every belt) has a shiny side and a suede side. If you fold and coil the belt as shown, the shiny side (marked A) will be the middle of the coil, and a pencil inserted at A will catch the belt when you try to snatch it, right? Right. Even a sucker should be able to figure this out, so let your victim succeed once. Next time, he'll put the pencil at A again. What do you do? Simple. Before jerking the belt, just let the tongue end unroll one turn. Then grab the two ends and pull. Letting the tongue end unroll one turn automatically changes the center of the belt from shiny side A to suede side B. Don't ask why. Just try it.

Of course, you may be working with a really dumb victim who can't even get it right the first time. In that case, now that you know the secret of switching the center

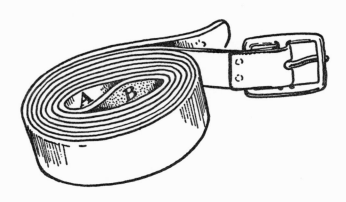

of the belt, you can rig it so he wins the first time. How many times you should let him win after that is up to your show-off conscience, and you probably know by now how hard-hearted that really is!

STRUTTING BEHIND
THE BUMBERSHOOT

April showers may bring the rain, yes, but they also bring you the chance to shine. You've seen this many times: some cool dude bopping down the street twirling an umbrella, sort of a drum-major marching to his own one-man band. This is further proof that showing-off can be achieved anywhere, with simple props, even in inclement weather. All you need for this is a standard-sized umbrella, rolled as tightly as possible. The tighter the roll, the easier it is to handle; for this reason, the British twirl umbrellas better than any other people. Class is a well-rolled bumbershoot; a well-rolled bumbershoot is perfect for gaining respect. Here's how:

Hold the umbrella in whichever hand is most comfortable. You should grip it between your thumb and index finger (figure 1), about one-third down from the handle. The trick is to move the umbrella from finger to finger, cradling it in the crotches between the fingers.

Figure 2 shows the umbrella after it has been passed from thumb-index to index-middle. This exchange is made smoothly if you rotate your wrist gently as you pass the umbrella along. Try it a couple of times; five minutes is about all you need to get it down.

Figure 3 illustrates a slightly trickier exchange. You must get the umbrella over your index and ring fingers, held there by your middle finger. Again, keep rolling your wrist gently.

This final exchange is completed in figure 4. While expert twirlers can now twirl back the other way, the beginner may stop here, grabbing the umbrella with the palm of the hand. A nice final touch is to flip the umbrella into the air, then pluck it out of the air with the palm of the other hand. Anyone can do that, of course, so it's no big deal unless you've twirled the umbrella first.

Twirling an umbrella is much like twirling a baton. Girls should have an easier time learning than boys. But girls have to put away their toys when they grow up. Boys, on the other hand, can look forward to a lifetime of twirling in the rain. We don't say that's fair. All we do is teach showing-off, and let society determine the rest.

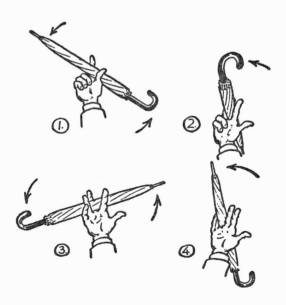

THE INVISIBLE
WRITER'S GUIDE

Everybody wants to be a spy. Most spies these days are sponsored by governments, and have access to fancy equipment that only governments can afford. But the most fundamental weapon that every spy needs is within the reach of anyone. You too, no less than the C.I.A. or James Bond, can be a master of the art of secret writing. Secret writing is useful not only for communicating secrets to other show-offs who know how to read it, but also for writing down secrets that are too important to be left to memory; like the funniest jokes, the best secrets tend to be forgotten.

Of course, you could write down your secrets in some kind of fancy code, but then you'd have to remember the code. The best way, therefore, is to use invisible ink in the first place.

Fortunately, invisible ink is at hand, right there in the kitchen or at the grocery store. Grab yourself an orange or a lemon, cut it in two, and squeeze the juice out. There's your ink.

Now, using some handy tool, write your message on a

piece of paper. The cheapest instrument for this purpose is a toothpick, but a wet toothpick only stays wet long enough to write about one letter at a time. Better, if you can find one, is a pen like the one illustrated; the best place to find one is an artists' supply store. Get a pen that will not scratch the paper you're using, thus giving the enemy a clue to the location of your secret writing.

On no account borrow somebody else's fountain pen, because lemon juice will really gum it up something terrible.

As you write your message in lemon juice, you'll notice that you can, if you look carefully, see what you are writing. But in a few minutes, after the juice has dried, no visible trace remains. There! Your secret is safe.

When you want your secret back again, just heat the paper. The safest way to do this is with a hundred-watt or so light bulb. Just hold the paper very close to the hot bulb until the writing appears. The paper should not quite touch the bulb.

If you're in a big hurry to read your invisible writing,

forget about the light bulb and heat the paper over a candle. Do *not* let it catch fire. When it's hot enough, the writing will appear out of nowhere, in brown ink.

If for some reason you can't find a lemon or an orange, milk will also work, but it's harder to write with and not quite so invisible when dry. Besides, an international spy carrying a milk carton is easy for the bad guys to spot, whereas the lemon in James Bond's pocket hardly bulges at all.

BLOWING OVER A WISE GUY

There's a big difference between a wise guy and a show-off. A show-off, as we all know, is someone who exploits his natural or acquired superiority to gain power and glory and recognition. Can you spot the show-off in the picture? Right, it's the piglet. A wise guy, on the other hand, is somebody who uses big words that nobody understands. People who own big dictionaries and know how to use them are wise guys, like the wolf here. The next time you meet a wise guy, the way to vanquish him is to say: "Hey, wise guy, I bet you get all your long words from a dictionary. Listen, wise guy, I bet you can't stand your big dictionary on end and then blow it over. I bet you fifty cents and the loser has to write 'antidisestablishmentarianism' on the blackboard a million times."

The wise guy, of course, will say it can't be done; or else, since a wise guy hates to lose, he'll take a little sissy wise-guy puff at the dictionary. This will be followed by bigger huffs and puffs, until he blows his face red and falls over in total failure, which is about to happen to the wolf.

Then what? The brave, intelligent little pig—the show-

off, of course—whips from his inside pocket a large paper bag, which he folds neatly and places on the table, as shown in the smaller illustration. Then he stands the dictionary up on top of the paper bag. Finally, he blows up the paper bag with his breath, in the ordinary way. The dictionary, naturally, topples with a crash. The show-off is victorious.

Remember, if you want to be a show-off and not a wise guy, the mouth of the paper bag must be placed close to the edge of the table so you can get your own mouth into position to blow it up. If you have trouble at first, experiment with the placement of the big book on the bag until you've got it right; then, go forth and knock 'em flat! Or if you want to pursue the luxury route, instead of a paper bag you can use a long, fancy balloon from the five-and-ten. Either way, you'll be out in front of the wise guys and running.

LOOK, MA, ONE HAND!

The show-off, always on the lookout for unique ways of impressing people, always asks whoever he meets to share any peculiar gimmicks, feats, or technical wizardry they might be hogging for their own personal glory. That's why we're able to bring you the wisdom of one Carmen Buccola of Garfield, New Jersey. Mr. Buccola, see, knows how to have a lot of fun with a bicycle wheel. It goes as follows:

Ask a chump if he can hold a bicycle wheel vertically with one hand—specifically, with one hand holding the wheel at the axle, as shown in the fantasy here. The chump will try it (which is why he's a chump in the first place) and find it very difficult indeed, no matter how strong he thinks he is. You then tell him you can hold the wheel at the axle, no matter how weak you really are. He laughs.

Then you have the last laugh.

The thing to do is grab the wheel with both hands, one on each end of the axle. Then—and this requires minimal practice—you give the wheel a strong spin with your finger tips.

When it's spinning vigorously, you can quite easily transfer the wheel to one finger and it will stay there, much as a toy gyroscope would. The wheel can even be balanced on the pinky. Mr. Buccola even claims a six-year-old child can hold it.

Our thanks to Mr. Buccola for sharing his special knowledge; if everyone would get up off his bicycle seat and show off just once a day, this world would be a better place for all of us.

STANDING AN EGG
ON ITS END

This wonderful stunt was contributed about five hundred years ago by Christopher Columbus, a notorious show-off who went on to discover America by sailing west until he fell off the end of the earth and landed here. One day Columbus and a bunch of the boys were whooping it up in a Seville saloon when Queen Isabella came in looking for her husband, a notorious rounder. Isabella had met Chris before because he was always asking her for money to fall off the earth with, so she went over to his table and asked if he could give her any information.

"Can I give you information!" Columbus cried. "I can even show you how to make a hard-boiled egg stand on end!"

"I bet you the *Niña,* the *Pinta* and the *Santa Maria* you can't," replied Isabella, forgetting all about her missing husband.

"Just watch," said Columbus smugly, and stood a hard-boiled egg on its end, right away, zip!

You can do the same stunt two ways. The modern way, which Columbus didn't know, is to pour a small heap of salt under the tablecloth, then replace the tablecloth and sort of scrunch the big end of the egg into that exact spot until a hollow develops in the mound of salt and the egg stands on end. If you do it this way you have to prepare the table in advance and not forget where the salt is. A brightly-patterned tablecloth helps to conceal the heap of salt.

But the old-fashioned Spanish way is simply to take the hard-boiled egg gently but firmly in your fist and bang its big end on the table until it's flat enough on the end to stand up. It's crude, but it worked for Columbus and it will work for you.

Queen Isabella was so impressed she coughed up the three ships without whining even once. Unless you can find a queen to astound with your eggmanship you'll probably have to settle for a smaller bet, but you'll win every bit as much admiration as Columbus did.

THE SAFETY-PIN SWIFTY

See how fat and happy this baby looks? That's because he knows how to perform a fantastic show-off stunt that nobody on his block can figure out—especially not his mother, his father, or his two bigger brothers. You too can be fat and happy until you grow up if you just get two safety pins and follow these instructions very carefully.

What you do is this: you walk up to your mother, your father, your big brothers, or a perfect stranger, and exhibit two safety pins, interlocked and closed. You simply grasp one of the interlocked safety pins in each hand and pull them apart, zip, just like that. You hand over the safety pins for inspection and they are both still closed. Amazing? Yes. Apparently one pin passes right through the other. Since it is the nature of safety pins to stay closed—that's why they're called safety pins—it's very hard to see how you pull them apart. In fact it's impossible.

That is, it's impossible unless you study, very carefully, the diagram of the two safety pins. Take two safety pins, the bigger the better, and interlock them exactly, that's exactly, as the drawing shows. There are about a hundred ways to interlock two safety pins and ninety-nine of them are wrong. Only the way shown is right.

Now, grasp pin A at the bottom in your left hand. Grasp pin B at the bottom—that's the head of the pin, actually—in your right hand. Pull A and B in opposite directions, as shown.

You'll find, if you're careful, that this set-up allows pin A to unlock briefly as pin B passes through its mouth. Then pin A snaps shut again, without any effort on your part. Practice this slowly at first, so you see how it works; then swiftly, so nobody else can see what happens. If you get stuck, you're doing it wrong. Remember, safety pins are only safe compared to normal pins—don't forget they're sharp. Use this trick to stick your friends and family, not yourself!

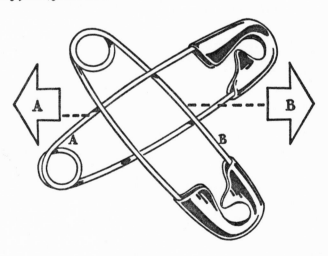

HOW TO PICK UP PEPPER
WITH YOUR WITS

As every show-off knows all too well, food offers a million ways to impress. Playing with one's food can be pretty awful—throwing peas, for example. But playing skillfully with one's food is an excellent way to score points. Consider the simple beauty of the feat we're about to show you: pick up grains of pepper without touching the pepper. All you need is some salt and pepper, plus a pocket comb, preferably clean.

Let's reveal the trick, then discuss some possible uses. All there is to it is this: static electricity applied to a comb picks up pepper like a magnet. (But it will not pick up salt.) As every child knows, you generate static electricity by running a comb through your hair fast and furious. So put a comb in your pocket, call a friend, and propose you go out for a hamburger.

Once in the restaurant, take the salt shaker and sprinkle a pile of salt on the table or a plate. Then take the pepper shaker and sprinkle a generous portion of pepper over the salt. Your friend is sitting there watching, thinking you're a little nuts.

Now tell him you can remove all the pepper from the mixture without touching it. If your friend says, "Now, why would you want to do that in the first place?" simply look philosophic and say, "Because it's there." This won't impress him much but it will at least hold his interest for a moment or so more.

Take your comb and run it through your hair. Place the comb over the mixture and, Zap!, the pepper grains will leap up into the comb, while the salt crystals just sit there, as dumbfounded as your friend.

There are, of course, a million dumb variations. One is to pepper your food, then cry out, "Ouch! I've put on too much pepper!" Rather than use your fingers, you pull out your comb and despice your platter with the above-described technique. It may look pretty disgusting but showing-off sometimes involves the unsavory. We never promised you a spice garden, did we?

THUMB FUN WITH A PENCIL

Nothing could be more open, more aboveboard, more obvious to the casual eye than this simple shifty little number. And, fortunately for the show-off, nothing could be harder to repeat from observation, or better adapted to driving your friends and enemies nuts by trying it themselves. It's one of those casual gestures that manage, somehow, to look like something they're not. You'll find it so easy to learn that you won't believe in its virtues until you let somebody else try it, and watch him or her turn all thumbs right in front of your laughing face.

To start, simply take a pencil—a full-length pencil, not a stub—and hold it under your thumbs with your palms together, as in figure 1 (note that the illustrations are drawn from your own point of view, not that of an observer).

Your next move is to cross your left thumb under your right thumb, as in figure 2, taking care to keep the forks of your two thumbs as close to each other as you can. This will result in the pencil starting to rotate clockwise, as the fingers of your right hand begin to glide over the fingers of your left hand. Your left hand begins to turn slightly palm down, your right hand a little more so.

The third position is shown (naturally) in figure 3. The thumbs are now parallel. The pencil has rotated about ninety degrees, and is held tightly pressed between the forks of the thumbs.

Now: continue the motion, using chiefly your left hand. The left thumb curls downward, then forward, around the pencil, and carries the pencil with it, until, at the end of the motion, the pencil is held in the thumbs below the hands, as figure 4 shows.

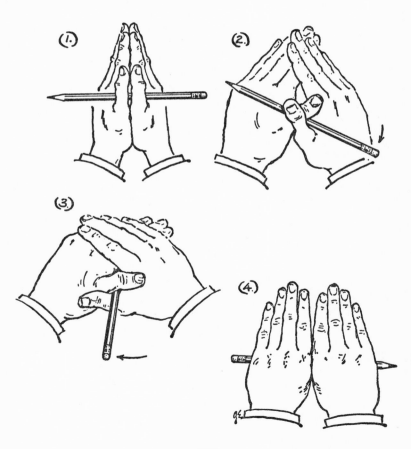

To reverse the motion, start by examining figure 5, which is shown as you would see it if you held your hands over a mirror. The thumbs are crossed—the right under the left—and the right thumb scoops the pencil off the left palm, resulting in a speedy return to figure 3. From here, just repeat the motion backward to figure 1.

Practice this until it all flows together in a single maddening motion. If you don't believe it's maddening, all right, don't believe! Just challenge a friend to do it with his own pencil, or better yet, a policeman with his nightstick. You'll find out, and so will they.

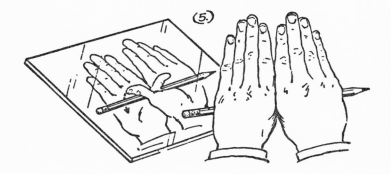

(5.)

A WALL-TO-WALL CARD STUNT

Here's the picture. You get locked inside a room with your opposite number. You're a buyer and he's a seller. Or you're a spy for us and he's a spy for them. Or you're a lawyer for the defense and he's a lawyer for the prosecution. Or whatever. Your negotiations have broken down—and nothing—reason, anger, even begging—can convince this guy that he's wrong. There's nothing that can break the stalemate.

So you order lunch and, while you're waiting for its delivery, you pick up a deck of cards. You walk across the room and, nonchalantly, start sticking the cards up against the wall. The cards stay there. Your opposite number, fast becoming your chump, stares. You are showing off. He is breaking down. He tries a few himself, like the fellow here on the right. The cards slide down the wall and collect in an embarrassing little pile on the floor. What's going on here?

This fantasy goes to show how subtle showing-off can be. Start carrying a deck in your briefcase (or school bag, or tote bag, or lunch box). When the going gets rough, find yourself a room with a carpet of synthetic fibers. Without a lot of fuss, shuffle your feet on the carpet, then gently place a card on the wall. It will stick. Then give the deck to your chump. He'll try to match you. His feet won't shuffle. His card will slide. And so on and so forth, bearing in mind it all works better on a dry day.

We all know that this same technique will cause balloons to linger on a wall, but only a show-off would think of applying the principle to playing cards. No, this knowledge will not rescue the world from tragedy. It will, though, rescue you from boredom or failure. Is that anything to scoff at?

BAUBLES, BANGLES
AND DIRTY TRICKS

For once, just for only once and never to be repeated, here's a show-off trick so low and rotten that it actually makes use of something up your sleeve. Most show-offs, most of the time, are too dignified and even honorable to make use of such a device; but there's a time for every-thing, sooner or later.

The time for this one is when you happen to own (or can buy reasonably cheap) two absolutely identical brace-lets, or a reasonable facsimile thereof. Little glass bangles from the dimestore will do fine. Of course, if you've got the class to own two identical expansion-band wrist watches, so much the better.

All right, put one of the bracelets (or wrist watches) up your sleeve—high enough to stick, but not so high you can't get at it in a hurry. Get a piece of rope two or three feet long. From here on out, just follow the pictures, like this:

Pick out some idle sucker who has nothing to do but let you deceive him. Walk up to him holding one bracelet and the rope and say, "Here, tie this rope between my wrists, and in the time it takes to say 'Harry Houdini,' I'll put the bracelet on the rope, which is obviously impossible, right?"

Your sucker, being able to see the obvious, agrees. Quick as a flash, before he can say even the first syllable of

DUPLICATE

"Harry Houdini," you turn your back on him, stick the bracelet in your hand deftly into some front pocket where it won't show, and slip the other bracelet off your wrist down into the middle of the rope.

If you're reasonably quick, you'll be finished long before your victim gets to the last syllable of "Houdini." But if you have trouble catching on at first, use "Bourke B. Hickenlooper" or "Department of Health, Education and Welfare" instead.

Part Six:
Cheap Thrills With
Real Money

THE PRANKY HANKY
COIN SNATCH

Making coins disappear is an indispensable star turn in the repertoire of every show-off. Of course, there are thousands of ways to make coins disappear, like swallowing them or dropping them down sewer gratings; but today's stunt is a lot niftier and less crude, and allows the performer to choose between just giving the coin back, or trying to outrun the original owner.

All right, here's how to pull it off. You need the following items: a small rubber band (the smaller the better); a big handkerchief (the bigger the better), or a scarf or dish towel; and a coin (borrowed from somebody who doesn't know any better).

Take the rubber band and wrap it around the fingertips of one hand, as shown in figure 1. The band should be snug, but not so tight that you can't easily wiggle it off your fingertips with a slight effort. Try it, and if it's too tight, get a looser band, or just wrap it around three or four fingers instead of five.

Holding the hand upright, drop the handkerchief over your hand so the rubber band is concealed. It will look like nothing more than an innocent handkerchief, right? Now, borrow the coin, tell your victim you're going to make it disappear, and stuff it, with your other hand, through the hanky into the middle of your rubber-band-wrapped fingertips, which form a sort of pocket to receive the coin (figure 2).

Everything should now be clear to you. You simply push the band off your fingers so it grabs the coin in the pocket. At the same time, you snatch the hanky into the air with your free hand, crying "Alakazam!" or some such. Of course, the coin and the rubber band cause a considerable lump in the handkerchief, so don't just stand there until somebody sees what's what; stick the hanky in your pocket right away.

It helps increase the mystery of this stunt if you already have a second, identical hanky in your pocket. Then, when you victim demands: "Hey, let me see that hanky," you can produce the innocent handkerchief and walk away with a smirk on your face and the coin in your pocket.

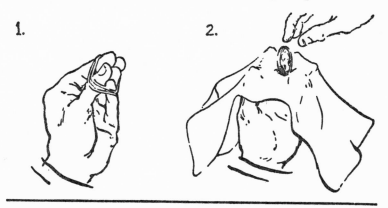

PUT A NICKEL IN THE SLOT

Next to actually owning a great deal of money, the best way to show off with cash is to make flashy exhibitions of what money you've got. Disappearing-coin tricks are especially appropriate if you're a little short this week, since with a bit of fast patter you can borrow somebody else's coin and then make it disappear where only you can find it—later, of course.

To make coins disappear, it is first necessary to practice palming for a while. Professional magicians can palm coins like nobody's business, showing you first one side and then the other of the hand that holds the coin, without ever letting you see it. You don't have to be that good to be a show-off, but you should be able to learn to hold a coin somewhere in the palm of your half-opened hand without dropping it or looking at it. Everybody's palm is different—just experiment with the lumps and creases in your own palm until you find your own spot. Walk around for an hour with a coin in it until you feel comfortable.

Now, borrow a coin from somebody and say you're

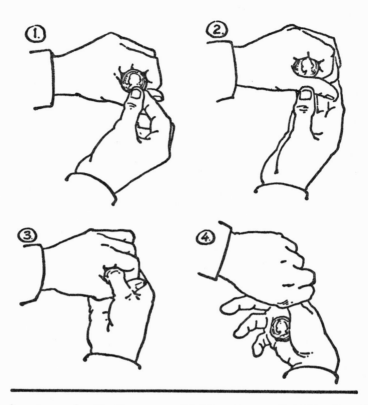

going to make it disappear. Hold out your left hand and make a fist, with the back of the hand upward. Leave a space in the middle of your fist about the size of the coin, and place the coin in it with your right hand (figure 1).

Position your right hand as in figure 2, and say you're going to push the coin into your fist until it disappears. When you're ready, push on the coin with your right thumb (figure 3). Note that your left fist is relaxed enough so that when the coin enters it, it's going to drop right on through into your right palm. The sucker who owns the coin, of course, is not going to notice this happening, especially if you're quick.

When the coin drops into your right palm, hold it there as you've learned to do (figure 4). Sweep your left hand into the air in an attention-grabbing manner and open it up with a cry of "Alakazam!" or "Zowie!" Remembering not to look at your right hand, stealthily get rid of the coin into your pocket.

Now, if you want to be a good guy and give the nickel back, that's your business—but if you don't, it's your nickel, if you're strong enough to keep it. That we can't teach you.

A QUARTER'S WORTH
OF DECEIT

The difference between a hard show-off trick and an easy one lies not in the skill required—anybody who can breathe in and out all day can handle the mechanical dexterity required for practically any reasonable stunt—but in the quality and quantity of the deception required to go along with the manipulation. Fortunately, ninety percent of showmanship lies simply in believing you're going to get away with what you're about to try; and if you didn't have that simple faith in your own superiority, that little voice inside your head that tells you you're a winner, you'd never be a show-off in the first place. Therefore, this lesson is slightly harder than most, but we've added a free extra simple trick at the end for those times when nothing seems to work for you. Start in on the hard part by plopping a quarter in the palm of your right hand and just looking at it for a moment, as in figure 1.

Reach for the coin with your left hand while turning the back of your right hand toward the audience—nothing obtrusive now, just a slight twist, enough to obscure their view of the coin a little (figure 2). Now, appear to grab the

coin with your left hand. Here's where belief in yourself
comes in, because you've got to make a tight fist around
the imaginary coin, while making a loose and flabby fist
with your right hand where the real coin remains.

Keep your eyes, and everybody else's attention, on the
left hand, and everybody but you will believe—such is the
power of suggestion—that the coin is in your left hand
where you're pretending it is. You can help out the illusion
by pointing at your left hand with your right, being careful, of course, not to actually let go with your right (figure
4).

Snap your left hand open. No coin! (figure 5). Everybody will think you've made it disappear and everybody
will fall down with admiration, provided you practice the
whole sequence of moves in front of a mirror until they
blend smoothly together, and also provided you really and
truly act as if you too believed you had transferred the

coin to the left hand. As soon as you can fool yourself, you're ready to go forth and perform.

Okay, that's the hard part. Now that you have it down pat, relax a little by pushing your quarter through a nickel-sized hole. Impossible, you say? We wish it were, because we still can't figure out how it works, and neither will anybody else you may be trying to impress with your command of spare change.

Anyhow, all you need to do is crease a piece of paper, then trace a nickel in the middle of the crease and cut out the hole (figure 1).

Try putting a quarter through the hole. Nothing doing, right? Very well, crease the paper as in figure 2 and drop the quarter into the hole, where it falls about half-way through. Then simply flex both ends of the paper upward a little (figure 3), the hole mysteriously elongates, and the quarter falls right through, plop. And plop will go anybody who told you it couldn't be done, especially if it was their quarter and you had a bet on it.

A MONEY-MAD
MANIPULATION

If you have wowed an assembled audience by rolling a quarter back and forth across your knuckles, and some wise guy asks you what you do for an encore, you, the show-off, better have one. Well, this is it. You will require nothing more than a few coins and your own fingers. The manipulation is a bit more difficult than rolling a coin across your knuckles, though it doesn't look like it. On this you're really going to have to practice. If you have trouble, don't blame it on us. We have tried it and it works. So there!

The problem is to hold four coins with your fingers and, using one hand only, reverse the order, putting the first coin at the end, then repeating the process again and again.

Figure 1 shows the correct starting position. You hold the coins with your thumb, index, and middle fingers. Hold them easily, without too much pressure.

The second step requires you to let the coin in front slide down a bit, your ring finger now coming into play

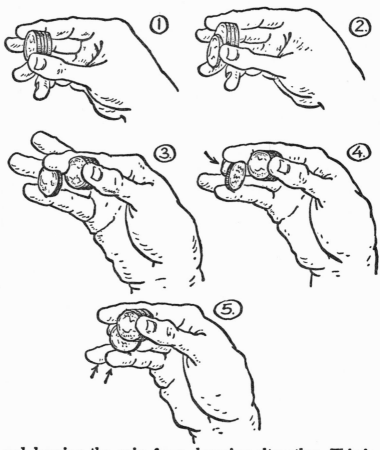

and keeping the coin from dropping altogether. This is shown in figure 2.

Figure 3 shows further progress. The coin you're moving is grasped between your middle finger and pinky, with the ring finger being cooperative and helping out as much as it can. What you want to do now is start revolving the coin back toward the end of the stack.

Figure 4 shows the proper direction. Begin to guide the coin toward your palm as the arrow indicates.

To avoid dropping the coin at this critical juncture, keep the coin propped with your pinky directly beneath it.

Keeping your hand and nerves steady as possible (watch it!), bring the coin back behind the stack and put it in place. Now you are ready to repeat the operation with the next coin.

Practice hard, maintain clean living, and have faith: if you do these three things—especially the first—you will soon be moving coins around with the agility of a Nureyev.

THE INVALUABLE
ONE-DOLLAR RING

Ken Geisel, a show-off from Clifton, New Jersey, goes around gaining respect and admiration just because he has this magic ring, see. Well, it's not really a magic ring, but it *is* made out of solid money and it's certainly worth its weight in cold cash. All you need to make it is a dollar and the manual dexterity of a six-year-old. If you're seven and have a fifty dollar bill, that's okay too—even better, in fact. No matter—knowing how to make a nifty ring out of a bill is a fine way to impress kids, also a surefire way never to be caught someplace with just lint in your pocket. Any cashier will gladly take this ring on your finger and give you a decent return in hock.

Take a nice fresh bill and place it in front of you (figure 1). Fold up the bottom edge, forming a lip with the bill's white edge, as in figure 2. Now fold the bill in half from the top down, tucking it under the white lip. Easy? Figure 3 points the way.

Figure 4 has you folding the bill once again, but this time don't tuck it into the lip. Just leave it cleanly folded.

Now you are about to turn all this folding into a ring

of proper size. Take the left side of the folded bill and form a ninety-degree angle (figure 5). Following the dotted arrow in figure 5, bring the right side around the vertical section, and stop when you're approximately 3/4 inch past it (figure 6). Make sure you are adjusting properly for the size of your finger.

Now, following the arrow of figure 6, fold down the vertical part and fold it up behind the face of the ring.

Take the 3/4 inch or so piece and bring it around in front of the face, tucking it in where shown (figure 7). This will keep the ring together. A little practice, and you will have the neat little item shown in figure 8. A dab of Scotch tape behind may be cheating, but it can help a lot.

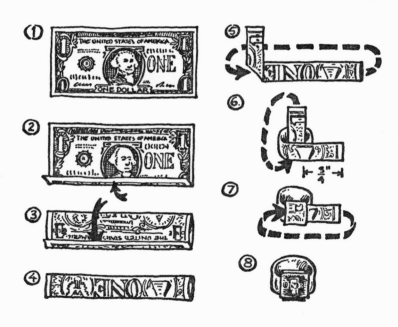

THE GREAT COIN CHASE

It's more important than ever these days to be able to keep track of your money. This stunt enables you to keep track of your small change with a feat of astonishing mentalism that may make your enemies so mad they'll throw anything that's loose—including their pocket money. You could clean up.

Here's what happens: you place three coins in a row and turn your back. You challenge a bystander to turn one coin over, then switch the coins around as many times as he likes, then turn the selected coin back the way it was. You take one look at the coins and tell him which he turned over. It never fails—provided you follow these instructions, and you can get your victim to follow yours. Here's how:

Take three coins of different values—say, a nickel, a quarter, and a dime. Write on a sheet of paper the numbers 1, 2 and 3 in a neat row, then lay out the coins below the numbers as in the illustration—all heads up. Put the dime on 3, as shown. Now you're ready to turn your back.

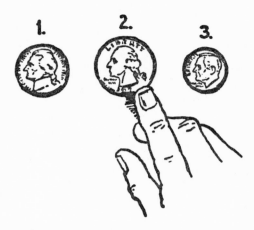

Remember, the dime is on 3. This is important! Got it? The Magic Number is 3!

Tell your sucker to turn any one coin to tails. When he's done that, tell him to switch the other two—the ones he did *not* turn over—with each other.

When he's done that, tell him to switch any coins with each other as many times as he likes—but he must tell you which ones he switched—1 and 3, 2 and 1, whatever, while you listen carefully.

Here's what you're listening for. You're trying to follow the transformations of your Magic Number—which was 3 to start with. However, if 1 and 3 are switched, the Magic Number becomes 1. Then if 1 and 2 are switched, it becomes 2; if 2 and 3 are switched, it's now 3 again; and so on. Got the idea? Just follow the number. It helps to use your fingers.

When your subject says he's switched enough coins, tell him to take the one he turned to tails and turn it back to heads. Now with your Magic Number, whatever it is, firmly in mind, turn around and look.

The first possibility is that the Magic Number has the dime on it. If this is the case, the dime is the coin that was turned over.

The second possibility is that the Magic Number does

not have the dime on it. If this is the case, then the coin on the magic number, whatever it may be, is *not* the coin that was turned over. The dime, wherever it may be, is also *not* the coin that was turned over. There is only one coin left, and *that* is the one.

There is no third possibility. It would seem that there should be, but there isn't, which is one reason this whole trick is so maddening. Can you figure out how it works? We can't, but show-offs don't know absolutely everything—just how to drive people nuts, and with this trick and three coins you're in the driver's seat.

A LINKUP IN SPACE

While Russian and American astronauts were joining each other in outer space a while ago, show-offs could only stand around with their hands in their pockets while governments got all the headlines. Here, now, for show-offs too poor to afford Apollo capsules, is a space-linking trick that will make you famous throughout the block you live on, and will only cost between one dollar and nothing at all. Besides, the dollar, if you have one, can be recycled for any use of your choice later on.

Your required astronaut equipment consists of a dollar bill and two paper clips. A strong piece of paper of the same size and shape can be substituted for the dollar.

Start by folding one-third, more or less, of the dollar behind the rest, as shown in figure 1. Then take one of the paper clips and put it over the fold, as in figure 2.

Still following figure 2, fold the left end of the dollar over to the right. Put the other paper clip over the new fold, as shown in figure 3. Note that the second paper clip is placed to the right of the first; also note that the second clip is placed only on the top and middle layers of the

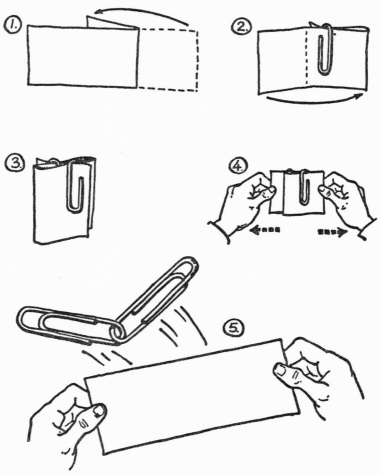

folded dollar. It does not, repeat *not*, fit over the bottom layer as well.

Now, grasp the two ends of the dollar and start counting down (figure 4). When you reach zero, pull the dollar out flat, as in figure 5. With a sharp click, the paper clips will spring into space, much harder than you probably think as you're reading this. What's more, they will be linked together, as the illustration shows. How come? That's classified information.

You can try this with additional folds and more paper clips on the dollar. About four is as many as there is room for, and they never fail to make the connection—sometimes in one long chain, sometimes in a sort of formless jumble.

If you could do this trick on the moon, the clips would fly four times as far, but that won't happen until the government recognizes the true importance of show-offs. Now that you know the techniques, getting the attention of the authorities is up to you.

THE FIVE-CENT SOLUTION

Otho C. Woods must be the biggest show-off in Whittier, California. Not long ago he sent us a nice letter in which he set down no fewer than eight sneaky feats, all of them worthy of your attention. Unfortunately, we only have room to pass one of them along. Total cost for props is five cents, for all you need is a nickel. And this is what you can do with the nickel. You can tell every time, even with your back turned, whether a nickel spun on a hard surface comes up heads or tails, just like the fellow in the drawing here is doing.

Mr. Woods's technique is so simple we're ashamed we didn't think of it ourselves. For this nickel business depends on a little nick, a nick you apply to the nickel with any hard material—a sharp stone, for example, or a file. Take the stone and etch a nick into the edge of the coin, either on the heads side (as shown in the inset) or tails, whichever you prefer. Now, in some very private place, where there is a hard-surfaced table, preferably one with a glass top, spin the nickel on its edge and, as the nickel slows down and begins to stop, listen very carefully. If the nickel falls on the side on which you've put your nick, it will give off a distinctly different sound than on the other, nickless side. You have to practice to hear the difference; it's a fairly subtle difference and practice is necessary for you to distinguish it. We can't really tell you what it sounds like, but, well . . . keep spinning that nickel and you'll hear what we mean.

Once you are able to hear the difference between heads and tails, go out and find your audience. Tell them you have psychic power to determine heads and tails. Take out the nickel from your pocket, turn your back, and tell them to spin the coin on the table.

With unerring accuracy, you will reveal heads or tails, much to the amazement of your fans. You might bet them a milkshake you can call the side twenty times in a row. And you can call it till the cows come home if you have that much free time.

THE INSIDE-OUTSIDE
COIN-AND-HANKY PASS

Here's a little number you can turn to when you're
down to your last nickel and clean handkerchief; those
with half a dollar and a posh restaurant napkin are not,
however, forbidden to play. The only thing that might put
you off is your sense of the fitness of things, what non-
show-offs call the Moral Sense. Since the illusion is
achieved by such a fundamentally dumb trick, you may be
ashamed to use it; but since it always works, you probably
won't.

What appears to happen is simple enough: you push a
coin right through a handkerchief, without making a hole
or even much of a fuss.

What really happens is even simpler. Just follow the
pictures. Start by picking up a coin between thumb and
forefinger of the left hand (figure 1). Now, drape a hanky
over the whole works *but*, as you do so, be sure to push a
little dimple into the top of the hanky, so a small fold is
caught between your thumb and the coin (figure 2).

Now comes the silly part. Flip back the front half of
the hanky, to prove the coin is still underneath (as the

arrow in figure 3 shows). Then, with a flick of the wrist, snap not only the front half of the hanky but also the back half forward over the coin (figure 4).

This looks as though, having exposed the coin, you're just covering it up again; but in fact, it results in more or less turning the hanky inside out, so to speak, so the coin is now held between your index finger and thumb, barely concealed behind the bottom fold of the hanky. The bulge at the top of figure 4 is the coin.

Now, twist up the hanky to show the spectator how tightly the coin is wrapped up in it (figure 5). When he's convinced, just squeeze the edges of the coin through the hanky, and it will squirt right out (figure 6).

Shake out the hanky to prove it is undamaged, and put the coin in your pocket. After a workout like this, you probably deserve it.

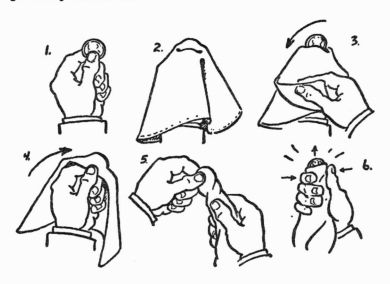

Part Seven:
Knot So Fast, Buster!

TYING A KNOT WITH
ONE HAND

Why should you learn how to tie a knot in a silk scarf with one hand, in a single deft manipulation? How can you ask? Everything you know how to do that nobody else can do is part of your show-off routine. How many of your friends, leaning against the candy store in midafternoon, can come up with anything as nifty as this? Be the first one on your block. And if you don't have a silk scarf, you can use a necktie or even, if worst comes to worst, a piece of string.

Here's how: Using both hands, roll the scarf loosely and lay it across one hand (we are using the right one for demonstration purposes), as shown in figure 1. If there's any difference in the length of the ends, the longer one should be toward you, on the front of your palm.

Now, clip the dangling end of the scarf, the one that's in front of your palm, between your fourth and pinky fingers (figure 2). Notice the end of the scarf marked A in the drawing. That's not the end you've grabbed with your pinky, it's the other end. Pay attention carefully to end A so you don't get lost in the next step. Ready?

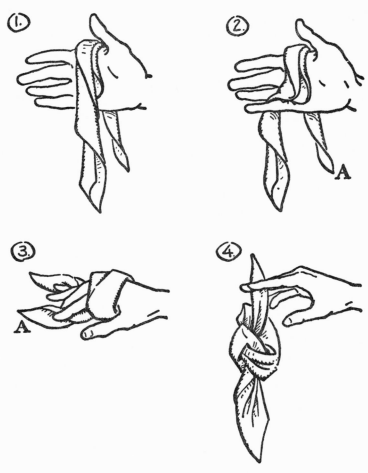

Roll your hand toward you so the palm goes down and the back up, until, with your index and middle fingers, you can reach around and grab the end marked A. When you've got it, you'll find that the scarf is loosely wrapped once around your hand, with one end of the scarf held between index and middle fingers, and the other between the fourth finger and the pinky. The scarf should be a loose fit on the hand, not a tight one. You are now ready to astonish yourself and others with the final step.

Let go with the fourth and pinky fingers. At the same time, keeping a firm hold at A with index and middle fingers, give your arm and wrist a snap downwards so the scarf falls forward off the hand. You now have figure 4, the scarf with a knot in it.

After a little practice, you'll be able to perform the whole number in a single swift motion. Then you can set out to amaze the neighbors, the candy store, finally the whole block. Tomorrow, the world!

SLIPPING THE CUFFS

The greatest professional show-off of all time, Harry Houdini, made his living by being chained up in handcuffs and ropes and so on and locked in trunks and dropped to the bottom of rivers. After a few minutes he would rise to the surface not only free and alive but dry all over. The average show-off can't do such heavy tricks and hadn't better try, but here's a dandy escape number to provide endless hours of entertainment for the show-off's friends and frustration for his enemies. We learned it from Bruno Profumo, an Englishman who passed through our country giving lessons in one-upmanship not long ago.

Take two people—a boy and a girl are best, for obvious reasons. Tie a piece of string two or three feet long between the wrists of one person; then tie a similar piece of string between the wrists of the other, being careful first to cross the strings once only, so the two people are linked together as in figure 1. Be careful not to tie the strings too tight, but tight enough so the hands can't slip out.

Now, challenge the two people to get out of this mess without untying the knots or cutting the string. Let them try. The more they try, the more fun it becomes. You'll get the idea after a few minutes of experimentation.

When they've had enough, refer to figure 2, which is drawn from the point of view of one of the two inter-

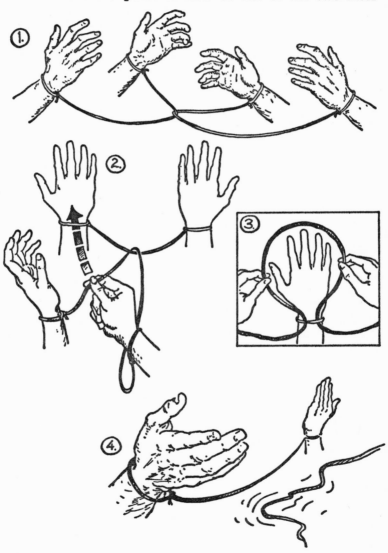

twined victims of this trick. Let one person just put his hands in the air and do nothing; the other grasps his own string at the point shown in the picture and inserts it up and under the loop around the opposite person's wrist, following the arrow.

Now the escapist pulls his own string upward through his partner's string into a loop, as shown in figure 3. He drops the loop away from him, over his partner's hand and wrist.

Both parties are now free, however unlikely this seems. They have only to spread their hands and step away from each other and zowie!—figure 4 results. If it doesn't, slash yourself free with a pair of scissors, go back, and follow the instructions more carefully, unless you want a new lifetime partner.

SPOOLING AROUND

Here's a work of great wonder that can be performed by any show-off with access to a sewing box. If you don't own a sewing box, you probably know someone who does; your mother will love you all the more when she sees what splendid things can be done with material ordinarily useful only for replacing buttons!

What seems to happen is: you present some spools, the ordinary sewing-thread kind, which have been threaded on two strings, as in figure 1. Any number of spools will do, from one on up, but we're showing three spools, a nice number to start with. You place a big handkerchief, a towel, or scarf over the spools, and mess around briefly underneath it (figure 2). Then, with a grand flourish, you jerk the strings and plop! the spools all fall off, but, amazingly, the strings are unbroken. Fantastic!

What really happens is shown in figure 3. Look carefully at the middle spool. As you see, the two pieces of string are not what they seem to be in figure 1. The trick is prepared by taking two pieces of string and tying them together in the middle with one tiny loop of white

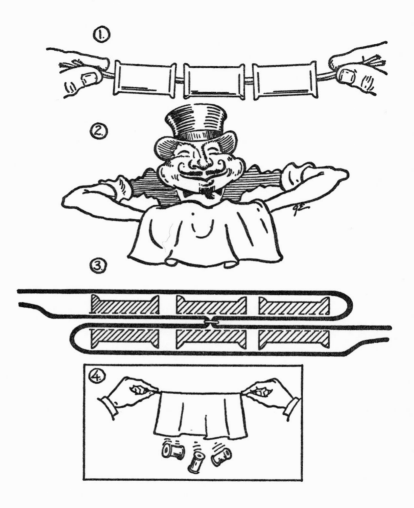

thread—there it is, right in the center of figure 3. The spools are then threaded on the strings so the whole affair looks like figure 1.

Now, drop the hanky over the spools—if you don't have three hands, you may want an assistant here—and simply switch the ends of the strings under cover of the handkerchief. The correct arrangement of the ends of the strings is shown in figure 3. The strings should be long enough so that they stick out from underneath the hanky when you're finished.

All right, now jerk the strings (figure 4). The tiny loop of thread breaks, the strings simply whiz out of the spools, and the spools fall free. You can even let an onlooker jerk the strings for you, as long as you don't let him peek beneath the hanky.

Hand over the strings to a spectator for inspection; the broken thread is so tiny it will escape notice as it falls to the floor. Give the spools back to your mother and bask in her attention as she tries to figure out where she got a kid as smart as yourself!

TYING ONE ON

Every show-off despises anyone who gets caught doing things the easy way when he could be seen doing them the hard way. The bow tie is a case in point. Anyone can wear a bow tie of some sort: there are clip-ons, snap-ons, probably even a glue-on somewhere. While these are certainly convenient, they are definitely not worthy of your respect, because the man who knows not how to tie a bow tie is a man without sunshine—or without something, we're not really sure what. In any event, hand-tied bow ties look more impressive than ready-mades, your selection is greater, and since it's easy to do in the first place, why not learn? Tying a bow tie is like tying your shoes—exactly. Follow these easy steps. Bear in mind the drawings represent your image in a mirror. That way it'll be easier to follow.

One end of the bow tie should start off longer than the other, as shown in figure 1. Take the left end and drape it an inch or so longer than the right.

Figure 2 has you bringing the left under and over; figure 3 shows you tightening the tie around your neck.

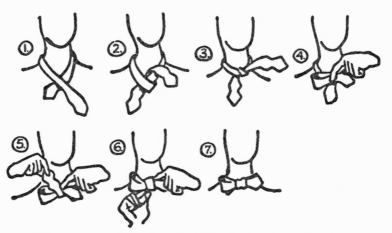

Using your right hand, fold the end you've brought under and over into what looks like the beginning of a bow tie, figure 4. Hold it there with your index finger.

Now with your left hand, take the end hanging straight down and bring it up and over the fledgling construction, figure 5. Keep a loop open with your right thumb.

The next step is a hard one, so listen. Your mission is to push the end you've just brought over through the loop being held by your right thumb. Just shove it through there and pull halfway through and as tight as you can, figure 6. At this point the knot is technically complete, but ugly and messy. Do not give up!

All that remains is the fixing up. Your bow tie is complete but a second or two of fiddling will make it straight and spiffy, figure 7.

Practice all this a few times and you'll hit pay dirt. Or learn how to tie your shoes and then apply that wisdom to your neck. Either way, your clip-ons and snap-ons will soon find themselves distinctly out of fashion. And it's about time.

KISS A STRING AND
MAKE IT WELL

In addition to nimble wits and lightning fingers, the show-off's most useful tool, when all's said and done, is his mouth. Today's stunt will show you how to perform a miraculous feat with, apparently, no other tool but your mouth—the bigger the better.

What appears to happen is that you approach a sucker, holding a doubled loop of string. You hold it out to him and ask him to cut it (of course you hope he's got a pair of scissors right there in his pocket). When he cuts through the doubled loop, you release one of the cut loops and stick the other in your mouth; then, presto, you pull the cut ends out of your mouth and they have, altogether miraculously, joined together.

Here's how it happens. Remember, we're showing it to you from your own point of view as you work it. Remember, also, we're showing you a great deal more of the trick than your sucker is supposed to see. This applies especially to figure 4, as you'll note when we get there.

Take a nice clean piece of string, maybe two feet long, and tie it into a loop. Give the loop half a twist forward

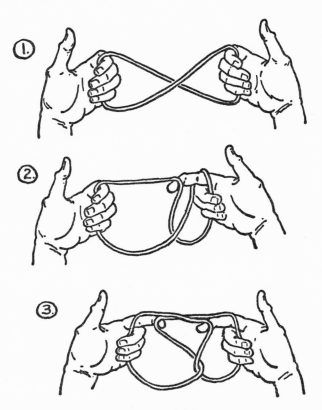

with your right hand and hold it in front of you as in figure 1.

Reach out with your right index finger and pick up the loop off your left hand (figure 2). Without dropping anything, now, reach out with your left index finger and pick up the loop off your right hand (figure 3).

See the sort of triangle opening up between your index fingers in figure 3? Reach in there with the remaining fingers of both hands and pull the doubled loop out. You now have figure 4, a double loop with the two loops joined as shown in the detail of figure 4.

Now then, the spot where the doubled loops are joined is the heart of the trick, and of course you don't want your victim to see it. Keeping it a secret is easier than it

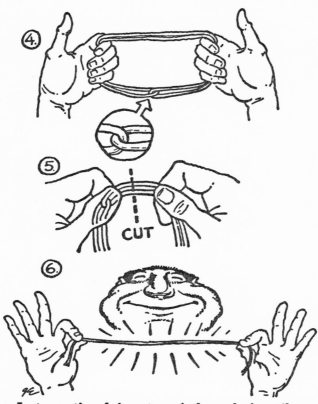

looks. Just practice doing steps 1 through 4 until you can
do the whole thing in a single flowing motion, too quickly
to follow. After all, you just say you're making a double
loop of string and then you make it. Just before figure 4 is
attained, you can "adjust" the loops by running the joined
spot in the string toward one hand or the other. It's easy
to get it out of sight behind one hand before you pull the
two loops snug. All right, practice for a while and then
we'll go on.

Ready? Keep on "adjusting" the loops until the spot
where the loops join is pinched between thumb and forefinger. Either thumb and forefinger will do—in our
example we're using the left (figure 5).

Now, being careful to hold your hands close together—

less than an inch, let's say—allow your victim to cut through the strings. Examine figure 5 carefully to see what's going on. It looks to him like he's cutting through two loops of string, but in actual fact he's cutting through one loop twice. Get it?

Let go with the hand that's not concealing the joint in the loops. You are now holding, in this case in your left hand, what looks like two pieces of string. Put them both in your mouth, joint and all.

Now you have only to mumble around with your tongue and teeth until you work the little remnant of the cut-off loop away from the wholly intact secret loop. Open your mouth and remove the string, retaining the little remnant until you can get rid of it safely. Presto! Healed string! You're a wonder! Collect your doctor's degree in oral surgery!

THE UNDERHAND
OVERHAND KNOT

All show-offs know how to tie an overhand knot in a piece of rope without ever letting go of the ends. Do you? If you think you do, get a piece of rope a couple of feet long, or a piece of string, or a rolled-up scarf or even a diaper, and try it for a while. Convinced?

All right, take a break. Stand around and lean on the wall a minute, and fold your arms as you relax. You know how people fold their arms when they're just standing around, right? You'd better, because that's the key to success. Just in case you have some doubts, simply put your left hand on your right biceps and then tuck your right hand between your left elbow and your chest. Your arms are now folded.

Now, get somebody to hand you the ends of your piece of rope, while your arms remain folded. Take one end in your left hand, which is easy; take the other end in your right hand, but be sure you don't move your hand to take it. You must grab the rope with your right hand under, not above, your left arm.

All right, you now have your arms folded and the ends

of the rope in your hands. It remains only to unfold your arms without letting go of the rope. You can cry "Alaka-zam!" if you wish, but whether you do or not, a perfect overhand knot will appear in the rope as you unfold your arms.

If you have no friend to hand you the rope, it's possible to manage by putting the rope on a table and then bending over, arms folded, and picking up the ends by yourself. As soon as the neighborhood knows what you're up to, friends will come running.

STRUNG UP BY
THE BUTTONHOLE

There are a thousand mystifying tricks in the show-off's ball of string, and one of the best is this string maneuver we learned from Joseph C. Poley of Alden, Pennsylvania. All you need in order to do this trick is a shirt with at least one buttonhole in it and a loop of string about two feet long; please remember that the drawings here are only a sketch, and do not represent our opinion of what Mr. Poley really looks like.

Start in the position shown in figure 1, with the string loop stuck through your buttonhole and over both thumbs. Your mission, now, is to get the string out of the buttonhole without ever letting go of it. Try it for a while before you read the instructions. See the point?

All right, now proceed carefully or you may get tangled up and have to have your shirt slit off you. Be sure the loop of string is not twisted (see figure 1). Now, with your left pinkie, reach over to your right side and pick up the string behind your right thumb on your left pinkie (figure 2).

Do exactly the same thing with your right pinkie,

reaching over to just behind your left thumb and picking up the string (figure 3). By this point you should feel pretty helpless, but rescue is in your own hands; you have only to let go of the string with your right pinkie and your left thumb. Now separate your hands (figure 4) and the whole thing slips from your buttonhole like a garter snake heading for the high grass, ZIP!

A word of complicated warning here; the illustrations are meant to show you how this trick will look to an observer, not how it will look in the mirror. However, like so many things in life, if you do it exactly backward it will work every bit as well. Also like so many things in life, you get much faster and better at it after a little practice.

THE FOUR-FINGER ESCAPE

There are lots of handy tools for the show-off to establish his superiority with, but none more handy than the everyday common piece of string. Others may be rich, wise, powerful, ostentatious—but as long as the show-off has even a piece of string, he can do something others can't. Even a couple of shoelaces might work, in a pinch.

In the Four-Finger Escape, the performer, or exhibitionist, takes a loop of ordinary string and wraps the fingers of one hand up in it. He winds the string around his thumb, and then wraps up his fingers some more. Then, with a dazzling flash and a superior smile, he pulls on the string and it comes free. To all appearances, the string has metaphysically passed through the fingers. Or did the fingers pass through the string? How? Well, it's all in the wrapping. Follow the instructions very very carefully, or you'll truss your hand up like a cat in a knitting basket.

Start the Four-Finger Escape by tying about a two-foot piece of string in a loop. Hang it over your left little finger as shown in figure 1.

Now, starting from your little finger, wrap the loop

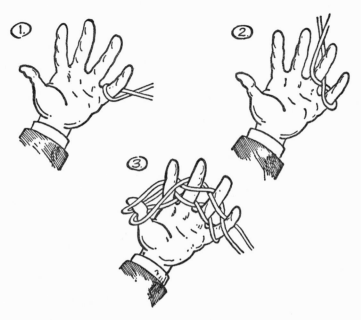

around each finger in turn, as shown in figure 2. The loop gets a half-turn to the right every time it goes around another finger. Continue until you reach the forefinger; then, without any further twisting, bring both strings around the thumb from back to front, as shown in figure 3.

Cross the forefinger again and go back toward the pinky, this time giving the loop a half-turn to the left at each finger. When you are finished, your hand should look exactly like figure 3. Study your hand and then study figure 3. Got it? If not, go back and start over.

When your hand agrees with figure 3, you're ready to escape. Just slip your thumb out of the loops by wiggling it a little. Then, pull with your right hand on the end of the string, and, with a mysterious motion, the string will slip right through the remaining fingers and you're free.

Part Eight:
The Power To Cloud
Men's Minds

ABUSING THE IMAGINATION

One way the show-off can triumph is by exploiting the outer reaches of man's brain, that small corner of his head where his imagination lies. The stunts we're about to show require lots of imagination but very few props: a cloth napkin, a paper bag, a thread that does not exist, and a rubber ball that doesn't exist either (using props that don't exist is a great way to whip inflation).

Take, for example, the cloth napkin. In figure 1, the show-off holding the napkin has just said to the chump behind him, "Watch this. I will take this napkin and, with my fingernails, pick loose a thread from the weave and pull it out tight with my left hand." The man makes a few "attempts" to free such a thread (though he's actually engaging in clever misdirection, one of the show-off's great allies). He eventually "finds" a thread and pulls it loose. The chump can't really see it but assumes it's too thin to perceive with the naked eye—and that, friends, is what makes him a chump.

The show-off holds the napkin in his other hand, as shown in figure 2, cleverly concealing his thumb in the

1.

2.

3.

folded corner of the napkin. He coordinates the hand holding the "thread" with the wiggles of the thumb holding the napkin. When he pulls the "thread" the napkin moves with it. The effect is this: the chump gapes as the show-off manipulates the napkin to and fro. It's a wonderful ice-breaker at lunch or dinner.

A suggestion for advanced show-offs: After you have found the imaginary thread, try sticking it in one ear, then pulling it out the other. This way when you pull the thread you will be pulling it back and forth through your head—and the napkin will wiggle-waggle just as easily.

In figure 3 you see a man about to catch an imaginary ball in a brown paper bag. Whaat?! Here's the pitch: bounce a nonexistent ball several times. Then, as you hold a paper bag between your thumb and fingers—make sure you turn down a lip on the bag as shown—prepare to flip the ball up into the air. As the ball "descends," move the bag under it. When the ball reaches the bag, snap your fingers hard, making the bag go Pop!—just as it would if a real ball had actually fallen into it. The resulting illusion is wondrously convincing.

OFF TO PHONE THE WIZARD

James Weaver, an art teacher in North Versailles, Pennsylvania, has this friend, see, a Wizard he calls from time to time. The Wizard has special powers of the mind—he can tell over the phone what card somebody holds in his hand miles away. Mr. Weaver puts a call in to the Wizard whenever he's in the mood to show off. He has most graciously decided to tell us—and you—the Wizard's phone number. Well, not really. Not actually the phone number but the low-down, inside poop on the Wizard. Here's how it goes.

Have a chump pick a playing card, any card, from a deck. Tell him you know this Wizard across town, a master of extra-sensory perception. The Wizard is so amazing he can identify the card over the phone. You dial the Wizard's number and say, "Hello. Is this the Wizard? (Pause.) May I speak to him then, please?" (Pause.) "Here he is"—and you hand the phone to your chump. The Wizard, speaking in a wizard-like voice, tells the chump what card he's holding. The Wizard then hangs up. Your chump drops his drawers.

Advanced show-offs may have already figured out that there ain't no Wizard, at least no Wizard with powers of

mind. What there is is this—your accomplice, a friend who can be counted on to play the Wizard whenever you have a chump on the line. This is how it works:

As soon as the Wizard hears you say, "Hello, is this the Wizard?" he begins to recite the suits: hearts, diamonds, etc. As soon as he identifies the suit of the card your chump is holding, you break in and say, "May I speak to him then, please?" Now the Wizard starts running down the card numbers: deuce, three, four, five, etc. When he gets to the correct card, you cut him off, turn to your friend, saying, "Here he is . . ." Your chump says hello. The Wizard tells him the correct card and hangs up.

Maybe you're wondering: What friend is so loyal as to play the Wizard any hour of the day, anytime it moves you to show off? You'd better be prepared to be his Wizard once in a while, even in the dead of night. It's the least you can do to gain glory.

HOW TO DRIVE A NEAT
PERSON CRAZY

The nice thing about showing off is that you can show off for everyone or show off for those certain types of people you think deserve a lesson or two. This trick will show you how to drive a very specific kind of person nuts, the thread-picker. You know the thread-picker—it's the person, man or woman (though usually a woman), who can't stand to see a piece of thread or lint or fuzz on your clothing. Nobody, of course, wants to have thread or lint on his clothing, but sometimes it's nonetheless annoying to have it picked off. This little ploy we're about to show you is the perfect comeback. It's an ancient ploy as timeless as the thread-picker himself (or herself).

The object in the box here is a flat sewing-machine bobbin, wound with whatever colored thread you like. What you do with it is this: Put the bobbin in the breast pocket of your jacket. Then, take the end of the thread and run it out of your pocket and through your lapel. Leave about an inch or so hanging out of the lapel. Then go to work or to school or to a party—or anywhere else you know you'll see friends, enemies and thread-pickers.

Sooner or later, somebody will be talking to you and they'll spy the thread on your jacket. When they do, just keep talking and stay cool. After a moment or so, the thread-picker will do her thing: she'll reach out, take the thread, and try to pick it off your jacket. She'll pull on it and more thread will appear. Then more. If she's compulsive enough, she'll pull at least a foot of thread before getting the idea.

She'll think twice the next time she tries to clean up your act.

HOW TO BE TELEPATHIC

Every so often the show-off leaves the real world of torn phone books and crushed beer cans and enters the mysterious world of psychic phenomena. And that, folks is where we're going right now. Fasten your seat belts for this amazing voyage through the brain, find an accomplice as well as a chump, plus nine ordinary playing cards, including two nines of any suit.

Inform your victim that he is to pick any of these nine cards and tell you which it is, and that you will "transmit" the identity of the card to the third person, your accomplice. You have, of course, previously arranged a deceptively simple ploy. Take a look at the drawing here. See the man touching a diamond on the nine of diamonds? That's you, and that's your ploy.

Your accomplice leaves the room. You lay out your nine cards in the H-pattern shown here. You ask your victim to pick a card—he picks, for example, the seven of spades. Your accomplice returns. You inform the accomplice that a card has been picked, and that you will concentrate hard on that card in order to send a psychic message. Then, starting anywhere you like, you go around the H-formation, touching each card and asking your accomplice, "Is this it? Is this it? Is this it?" And so on.

The key lies in the nines. For when you touch the first nine you come to, touch it on the figure that corresponds to the card in the H-pattern; as you can readily see, the spades or diamonds or hearts or clubs on a nine are arranged in the same H as your larger layout on the table. By touching the correct diamond you signal the placement of the chump's selected card—in this case, the seven of spades. You use two nines so that your accomplice can't fail to pick up your clue.

When the accomplice proclaims, "Yes, that's the one. That's his card!" your victim will be dumbfounded. He'll ask that you do it again. You do. You will feel the rush of supreme glory once again.

HIGH, WIDE HANDIES

There are many low forms of wit—puns, moron jokes, etc.—but the lowest and most annoying, without doubt, is the Handy. About every ten years a wave of Handies, those mysterious gestures that the show-off performs, and then invites the onlooker to guess what they are, sweeps the country. It's been several years since the last invasion, so the show-off is well advised to prepare himself now. Be the first on your block to have a ready repertoire of Handies, so that when conversation lags you'll have something left to say with the two paws nature gave you!

Figure 1 shows how the Handy works. At a critical moment in midoperation, the famous surgeon drops his tools, joins his right forefinger and thumb together, wiggles the other fingers furiously, and sweeps the whole gesture in a wide arc from his left to his right. Just when the bystanders notice there's something wrong, the famous surgeon demands: "What's this?"

Naturally, nobody knows what this is. With a shout of triumph, the famous surgeon exclaims: "I don't know either, but here it comes again," and repeats the gesture.

All the bystanders faint—some with admiration, others with outrage. To the show-off motivation doesn't matter, as long as they react!

Now, try figure 2. Place the palm of one hand on the back of the other, rotate the thumbs madly, and sweep the whole affair forward gracefully through the air. Shout out: "What's this?" "We don't know," the world will reply. "A duck with automatic transmission!" you exclaim. Groan!

Figure 3 shows both stages of the Handy you explain to an anguished audience as "A spider doing push-ups on a mirror."

Figure 4, the greatest of the classical Handies of the past, works like so: "What's this?" you demand, showing your palm up with the fingers slightly curled.

"I don't know," your victim confesses as he grits his teeth.

"THIS, DEAD!" you snap as you exhibit the same gesture right-side-up, so to speak.

From here the show-off proceeds to create Handies of his own. For example, use a gesture of your own invention and ask what it is. When they give up, declare it's "elephant repellent."

"There are no elephants around here," they're sure to object.

"You see, it works!" you cry, and start running.

HOW TO BE AN EASY ACE
AT TENNIS

Let us begin by admitting the best way to show off is to be actually good at something. The surest way to glory and success is skill. But since not many of us really have skill, it might pay to start looking around for what's second best. What's second best is style. For even if you do things lousy, you can always score a few points with your style.

Perhaps, for example, you sometimes play a little tennis. If so, chances are you are an average weekend tennis player. This means that for every set you win, your opponent wins a set. And for every easy slam you sock into the net, your opponent will sooner or later match you.

Such play is fun, no doubt, and certainly good exercise. But don't you sometimes get impatient? Don't you sometimes want to look better than your skill allows? Some players try to look better by buying expensive tennis outfits and shiny steel rackets. Our suggestion is more subtle. Try showing off by knowing how to pick up errant balls without bending over. This gives the impression you are being casual about the whole affair—and makes losing a lot less embarrassing. Below are two easy ways of being graceful on the court, a lot more graceful than any of your shots.

Side-of-the-foot method: The duffer you see here is about to pick up a ball with his foot. He has just fanned on an easy lob and checked out his racket for holes. Now he will recoup. He walks over to the ball and, using his racket, rolls it up to his foot. He keeps the racket against the ball and, in one graceful lift, brings the ball up between racket and foot. With a deft kick, the ball is popped into the air, and the player catches it nonchalantly with his free hand. The ball is now in the hand used to toss it up for serving. That's it. One easy motion, no bending, no sweat. The player might now strike a yawn to enhance the effect.

Shovel method: Another way to pick up a ball is to shovel it with your racket. The three drawings here show the important steps. Place your racket over the ball, as in

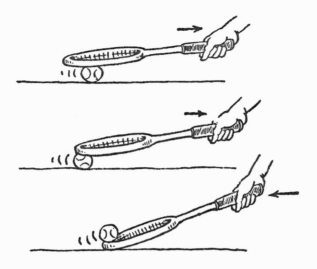

the top drawing. Pull your racket toward you with a quick jerk of the wrist, as in the middle drawing. This action permits you to then get your racket under the ball with a quick forward motion of the wrist (see bottom drawing). Now all you need do is flip the ball into the air and catch it with your free hand.

HOW TO MUG YOURSELF

An infallible way to get other people's attention is to commit violence on them. Nobody can ignore you if you kick them in the shins. The trouble with showing off by hitting people is that if they're big and powerful they hit you back; and of course it's exactly the big and powerful whose attention the show-off most desires.

A much safer way to make everybody look at you is to commit violence on yourself. You probably already know how to crack your knuckles, for instance, and you know how impossible it is for anyone to ignore knuckle-cracking. Well, the same goes in spades for the art of nose-cracking. Get a grip on your proboscis and hang on while we tell you how to do it.

Here's the effect: after announcing that you're about to break your nose, stand and face your audience. Look them in the eye, and place one hand on either side of your nose, as in figure 1. You bend your nose a little to the right, then a little to the left, just to loosen it up, you say. You give it maybe a couple more flexes to get it nice and soft. Then you twitch it firmly to one side or the other—

always leaving your hands in place—and it emits a loud, sharp CRAACK! You'll never know till you try it how sick this will make everybody watching. They'll beg you never to do it again! Of course, you do it again, right away.

So how do you do it? See figure 2. The actual noise of flesh and bone splintering is made simply by dragging your thumbnails across the edge of your front teeth with a sharp snap. Of course, in real life the position of your hands conceals your thumbnails so people think it's really your nose breaking off. The longer your thumbnails, the louder the noise.

On your way out of the room you can make everybody feel a lot better if a mysterious hand grabs you by the throat and gives you the punishment you deserve. The mysterious hand, of course, is yours, cleverly arranged, as the picture of the man in the doorway shows.

THE MYSTIC MAGNETIC
SEX DETECTOR

See the bald-headed mad scientist in the picture? Like all show-offs, he's using his secret powers to baffle and astonish other people by pulling stunts they can't understand. In this case, he's demonstrating how the sex of a human being can be determined by using the Mystic Magnetic Sex Detector—which is nothing more than a ring (or any other small weight) attached to a couple of feet of ordinary string.

Of course, the Mystic Magnetic Sex Detector isn't really mystic, and it isn't magnetic either. What it is, is an age-old demonstration of the fact that beliefs can influence actions, even unconsciously.

Here's how it works: you suspend the ring over the palm of a human being of either sex. Then you set the ring to swinging in a gentle arc. If the palm belongs to a female, the swings of the ring will, after a few seconds, settle into a circular pattern (figure A). If, on the other hand, the subject is male, the ring will soon begin to swing back and forth, more or less in a straight line (figure B). That is—and

287

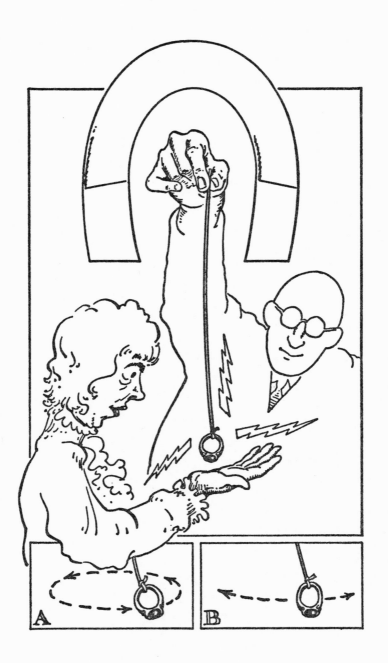

this is very important—the ring will do this if you believe it will!

Why is this? Because, no matter how hard you try, you can't hold your hand perfectly still—it always moves a little. What's more, the movements of your hand will be affected—whether you try or not—by your own expectations. If you believe it will go in a straight line, for boys, or a circle, for girls, it will. If it doesn't, you must not be paying attention.

Since this test works so well for human beings, you might well imagine that it's been tried on more difficult subjects—like eggs, for example, to see what kind of chicken will come out. Well, it has, and it doesn't work—sorry. So long as you confine your demonstrations to people, you can make it happen for yourself, or anybody else who'll believe that what's going to happen is going to happen. We leave the persuasiveness—something every show-off needs lots of—up to you.

THE INDIA RUBBER PENCIL

A show-off's whole career is based on creating one big illusion—making people think you're smarter, more graceful, and more accomplished than you actually are. Such an illusion, if persisted in, becomes true in the long run, especially if you begin to believe it yourself. But like all big illusions, it's made up of a lot of little illusions. Watch this one carefully, please.

Nothing can make you feel more powerful than making people see things that aren't really there—pink elephants for example, or flying saucers. Pink elephants and flying saucers are hard to conjure up; but India rubber pencils are all over the place, waiting for you to create them. To make one, start with the ordinary pencil of your choice, the longer the better; no stubs, please. Better yet, borrow a pencil from the nearest available victim, hold it up in front of his face, and tell him you're going to turn it to rubber. This he won't believe, take it from us—at least not until, with a few deft wiggles of your accomplished hand, he sees the pencil flex up and down like crazy—or like rubber.

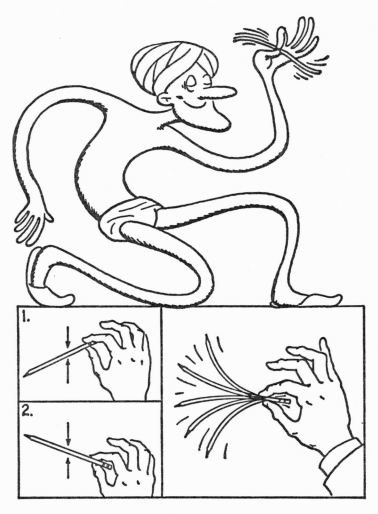

How is it done? It's all in how you wiggle the pencil. Hold it loosely by one end, between forefinger and thumb, as shown in figures 1 and 2. Note the arrow pointing to the center of the pencil. Now, as you wiggle the pencil up and down, holding it loosely, your hand rises and falls in the identical but opposite rhythm. Figure 1 shows the top of the stroke, figure 2 the bottom. Try it; you'll get the hang of it in about a second.

The third drawing shows, not what actually happens, but what a spectator sees—or thinks he sees. The whole effect is owing to persistence of vision, the same phenomenon that allows you to see, among other things that aren't really there, movies that seem actually to move.

Once you've learned to make rubber pencils, it's up to you to find uses for them, like signing checks that are going to bounce anyway. Just don't stick them in your ears.

Part Nine:
Looky What You Made!

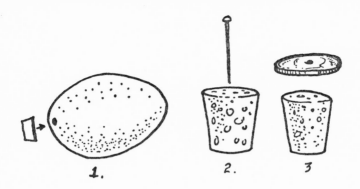

1.   **2.**   **3**

THE EGG ROCKET

One of the first show-offs recorded by history was the Greek physical philosopher Hero of Alexandria, who may have lived as early as the second century B.C. He invented the very first jet-propelled device, the aeolipile, which ran round and round like crazy, driven by jets of expelled steam, without ever getting anywhere. To make your own name famous forever, like Hero's, it is only necessary to construct this modern jet-propelled equivalent of his invention.

Take two eggs, and extract their contents either by (a) punching one tiny hole in one end of each egg and sucking out the egg, or (b) punching one tiny hole in both ends of each egg and blowing them empty. Method b is easier, but if you use it you must seal one hole with a small square of aluminum foil and some kind of glue that will resist heat and dampness (figure 1); Lepage's Liquid Solder is good for this purpose (although not perfect; follow instructions on the tube and hope for the best).

Take a large cork and drive a large pin or needle right through the middle (figure 2). Stick a couple of small forks

firmly into opposite sides of the cork and then, carefully, using soft copper wire from the hardware store, suspend the eggs from the ends of the forks and a pair of metal thimbles below the eggs. Your final product will not be as neat as this drawing may lead you to think is possible; don't worry. Just wrap everything up in copper wire until it's secure.

The eggs should be firmly attached to the ends of the forks and the thimbles solidly suspended below the lowest points of the eggs. Be sure that the open holes in the ends of the eggs face in the same angular direction—i.e., either clockwise or counterclockwise. Now, lay this assembly aside for a moment.

Finish the main bearing for the machine by drilling a

small hole about halfway through a penny, for the end of the needle to rest in. Now, either glue the penny directly on the mouth of a large, heavy bottle—too large and heavy to tip easily—or glue it to a cork that fits the bottle (figure 3).

Assemble the machine, now, by placing the egg-and-fork structure carefully on top of the bottle and bearing. Very likely it will tilt to one side, out of balance. Adjust the balance either by pulling out one of the forks and replacing it in the cork, or by wrapping more wire around the end of the lighter fork, or both, until the balance is achieved.

To load the rockets, it's necessary to get some water inside the eggs. This is hard! Use a fine-pointed eye-dropper, a model railroader's oiler, or a model builder's glue gun to get maybe a half teaspoon of water inside each egg. When you're convinced there's some in there, stoke the thimbles by stuffing them lightly with cotton, then soaking the cotton with denatured alcohol. You may be tempted to use lighter fluid, but don't; it smokes something awful.

Take the whole contraption to a safe place, like a big tile bathroom or a concrete basement floor, far, far from anything that might catch fire. Assemble the machine and recheck the balance, adjusting as necessary. Finally, light both thimbles with a match.

After a few minutes, the water in the eggs will begin to boil, and steam will rush from the holes in the eggs, causing the whole thing to spin madly with a great hiss. Ours attained about forty revolutions per minute at top speed; yours may do better. Warning: if you let the eggs run dry inside, the glue patching the sealed pair of holes will fail and you'll have to start all over again.

Once you're convinced it works, call in any jet pilots who live in the neighborhood and astonish them by doing anything they can do, with the help of two eggs and the will to show off.

A HANKY IS A HANKY
IS A ROSE

If you're respectable enough to carry a handkerchief, you can be even more respectable after we tell you how to take an ordinary pocket handkerchief (a clean one, please) and form it into a rose of unspeakable beauty. Remember this the next time someone of the opposite sex asks for your hanky. Instead of giving her a plain handkerchief, give her a veritable flower.

Take your square handkerchief and, as in figure 1, fold over a corner to the middle. Repeat this folding for each of the corners and you will wind up with a newly-formed square.

Do exactly the same thing once again, a folding process that will yield the form shown in figure 2.

And repeat still another time. Figure 3 shows the same folded hanky, this time one step smaller.

Now take your folded handkerchief and turn it over. Fold the corners the same way as before, as shown in figure 4.

Pick up the hanky by the pointy part (figure 5) and turn it over, palm of your hand facing up.

Now gently pull out the "petals," making a blossoming, fluffy flower. Your final rose should look as wonderful as the one in the drawing (figure 6).

DINNER MUSIC FOR THE SPOON PLAYER

The true show-off can never be quiet, lest the attentions of his admirers should be drawn to something even more attractive than himself. Almost any time is a good time for the show-off to make a noise, but one of the best is whenever he can add himself, as a private rhythm section, to whatever music is coming in through the radio or over the juke box.

Gil Eisner, the artist who illustrated this book, learned to play the spoons while in the Army. His fancy jug-band rat-a-tats earned him many friends and many extra turns at K.P. Here is his easy method for becoming the best musician in any kitchen on your block.

Get a couple of big spoons. Not just any spoons will do—they should be slightly reverse-curved at the handle ends, so the handles will bear nicely on each other when the spoons are held in the fist (see figures 1 and 2).

Spoons shaped for eating are not necessarily the best ones for sweet music. In figure 1, the top spoon is shaped the way it comes from the spoon factory. For performance purposes, bend the bowl of the spoon down, maybe fifteen

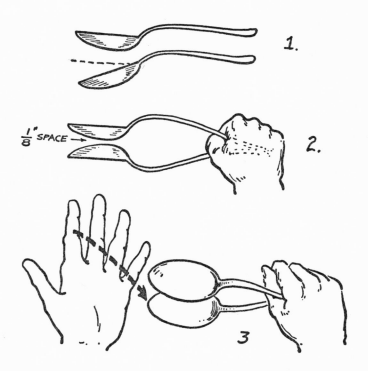

degrees, as shown in the bottom half of figure 1. Treat the other spoon likewise. It is best not to do this with your mother's good silverware. Use something cheap from the dime store.

Grasp the spoons gently but firmly in your fist as shown in figure 2, with one handle passing above your thumb and one below. The handles of the spoons should be in contact inside your fist, the bowls of the spoons about an eighth of an inch apart.

All right, now softly bop something with one of the spoons. Notice how the bowls come together with a sharp plunk, then spring apart ready for another plunk? There is your basic spoon rhythm stroke. Now turn on the radio and listen for something to join in with. All kinds of elegant variations are possible, as you pass the dancing spoons over the backs of your knees, the top of your head, and wherever. The basic riff, of course, is derived by rippling the spoons across the four fingers of your free hand, rattlety-plunk (figure 3). Now all you need is some friends with washboards, jugs and maybe a bass fiddle and you're on your way in the footsteps of Mozart, Beethoven, and Taj Mahal.

THE BETSY ROSS
FIVE-POINTED CAPER

Now that our nation has arrived at its Bicentennial, show-offs rejoice to remember that the United States is the greatest show-off country on earth. The legend of showing off in America records this topping stunt by Betsy Ross, maker of our first flag: when George Washington went to call on Betsy Ross to ask her to make a flag, he presented her with a sketch of what he had in mind.

"All the stars have six points," said Betsy.

"So what?" said George.

"Five points is prettier," she replied.

"Yes," said George, "but six points is easier to make."

"Not for me!" cried Betsy, and showed off then and there by snatching a piece of white cloth, folding it a couple of times, and snipping once with her scissors to produce a perfect five-pointed star. And that's why we have the flag we have today, instead of one less pretty. Now here's how Betsy did it. Get a piece of paper (or cloth) and a pair of scissors and be like her.

Take a piece of paper—8-1/2 by 11 typing paper is fine—and hold it vertically as in figure 1. Fold once in half (figure 2). Now, take what you have after performing figure 2, and make a mark at the midpoint of the left-hand side (the easiest way to do this is by folding in half once more, as in figure 3, and creasing lightly just at the left edge, then flatten it out again back to the configuration of figure 2).

Fold the lower right-hand corner to the midpoint of the left edge (figure 4) and crease. Now, see figure 5; take the right-hand edge of what you made in figure 4 and fold it down and to the left until it too crosses the midpoint on the left along the new edge created in figure 4. Crease.

Now, fold the left bottom corner upward and crease as in figure 6.

With the scissors, cut along the imaginary dotted line shown in figure 7. Unfold the paper and there you have it. Repeat fifty times and you have enough stars for the whole country, including Alaska and Hawaii. If there are any states you don't like, you can leave them out.

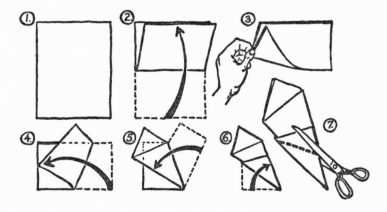

CURSE OF THE
COOTIE-CATCHER

The purpose of the cootie-catcher—a folded-paper gadget formerly found in every American third-grader's school desk but now falling into disuse—is to stupefy your friends by showing them that their hair is full of little black bugs, or cooties. What you do after that depends on how fast you can run, or how good your friends really are. A reasonably adept show-off should be able to handle the consequences gracefully. Now, here's how to handle the preliminaries, by making a cootie-catcher.

Take a full-size sheet of typing paper and fold one corner over to the opposite edge to make a square (step 1). Cut or tear off the remainder, keeping the square part (step 2).

Lay the square flat and fold each corner to the exact center of the square, creasing each fold (step 3). Turn the result over, and fold each corner to the center of the square again (step 4). Crease the folds firmly.

You now have step 5, and from here on out is where you have to be careful. You need two more sharp creases, vertical and horizontal, which you get simply by folding

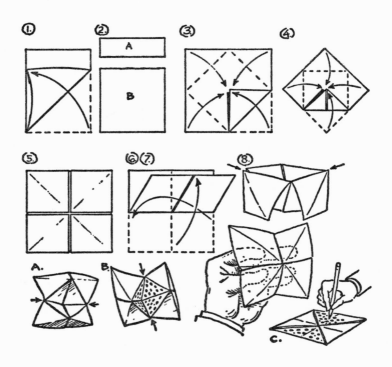

step 5 in half—first from top to bottom, then from side to side (steps 6 and 7). In each case, make a sharp crease, then return to step 5.

Now, take the step 5 object, suitably creased, and push, do not fold, two opposite corners toward each other, as the two arrows show in step 8. The whole thing should snap into a sort of crown-shaped affair, with triangular corners, into the back of which you can insert your thumb and fingers as the shadow-line drawing below step 8 shows. One finger to each corner, except that your fourth and pinky fingers go together.

You are now almost, but not quite, ready to catch cooties. Study the method of operation of the completed cootie-catcher, as shown in figures A and B. Notice that the cootie-catcher is hinged in two planes at right angles to each other (see the arrows in A and B?). You approach a victim holding it open, as in A. You clap it swiftly to his head and exhibit the result, as in B. Ugly black dots all over! Argh, you cry, an infestation of horrible cooties! Off to the showers with your friend.

Where do the ugly cooties come from? Pen and ink, is where. Just for a moment, return the whole device to the configuration shown in step 5. Now, referring to figure C, put nasty black dots all over two opposing faces of the cootie-catcher. Now put it back on your fingers, and you'll find it's easy to show whichever pair of faces you want to show—with cooties or without. Go forth and diagnose the cooties in your classroom, office, or, best of all, your barber shop.

UP AND DOWN WITH THE CARTESIAN DEVIL

The nasty little creature in the picture, with the long tail and the diving mask, is not really the hero of this chapter. The real Cartesian Devil is the gadget at his right— a gadget which has its place in demonstrating some laws of physics, but whose actual purpose is to enable you to baffle your friends with your cleverness by exerting your mysterious powers to make the floating eyedropper in the bottle rise, sink, or hover in the middle at your word of command. Of course, you have to cheat to make it happen, but you probably expected that.

To make a Cartesian Devil, get three things: (1) a clear, flexible plastic bottle of the kind that shampoo or dish detergent comes in; soak the label off; (2) a plastic eyedropper; (3) an inch or so of soft wire—plain copper is good, but soft solder is better, because it's softer.

Fill up the bottle with water. Wrap the wire around the end of the dropper so it will float in a stable position, end down. Now, put enough water in the eyedropper so that, when dropped in the bottle, it just barely, and we mean barely, floats. The rubber end of the dropper should

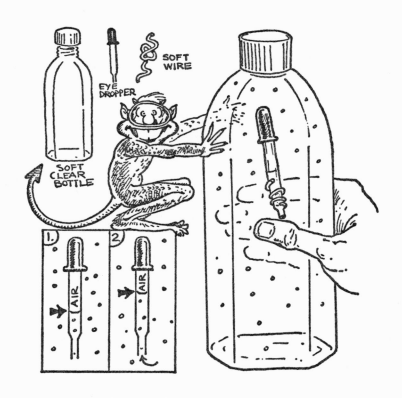

SOFT
WIRE

EYE
DROPPER

SOFT
CLEAR
BOTTLE

1.
AIR

2.
AIR

scarcely break the surface. Adjust the amount of water in the dropper until you have it right.

Screw the top on the bottle. You are ready. Pick up the bottle and give it a squeeze. Amazing! The eyedropper sinks to the bottom. Stop squeezing and the dropper rises.

When showing off in public, of course, you'll want to hold the bottle at arm's length, while making mysterious gestures with your free hand to convince the ignorant that your psychic powers are doing the trick for you.

What's really doing the trick for you? Glad you asked. Since air can be compressed and water can't, when you squeeze the bottle something has to give. And the only air in the bottle is contained in the top of the eyedropper. So the floating dropper (detail 2) becomes the sinking dropper when you squeeze the bottle, compressing the air in the dropper and causing more water to enter through the hole in the bottom (detail 2). The soft rubber bulb on the dropper has nothing to do with the case, it's only a convenient means of adjusting the amount of water in the dropper. So that's the theory. As for why the thing is called a Cartesian Devil, we don't know. If you're any kind of real show-off, you should be able to make up a story about it without any more help from us.

THE MOEBIUS STRIP TEASE

Germany is not a land notable for show-offs. Slow and steady is more the German style (though they don't mind making show-off equipment, like Porsche cars, for Americans). Nevertheless, the lightning from heaven that makes a show-off can strike anywhere, and one day in 1858 it descended on the mathematician August Ferdinand Moebius, who was sitting around his library in Leipzig cutting out paper dolls and such-like. Suddenly, Moebius rose like a shot from his armchair and cried: "Donnerwetter! I have invented a piece of paper like the world has never seen before. Fame and glory are mine!"

Moebius was right; he is now known worldwide for inventing the Moebius Strip, a piece of paper with truly astonishing properties. You can astonish your immediate vicinity by doing what Moebius did; simply take a strip of paper about two feet long (the long way of an unfolded sheet of newspaper is about right), give it one-half turn as shown at the top of the illustration, and tape or paste A to B, so as to produce a loop of paper with half a twist in it.

What is so remarkable about this loop? Well, for one

thing, it has only one side and only one edge, as you can easily prove by drawing a line down the middle until it meets itself. More remarkable is what happens when you take a pair of scissors and cut down the line, dividing the paper half-and-half. Go ahead. You were expecting maybe that by cutting one loop in two you would get two loops? No such thing! You get one loop twice as long as the one you started with!

More surprises are possible. Instead of making a half-twisted loop, give the paper one full turn before sticking the ends together. Then cut down the middle. Result: two loops all right, but interlinked. If you have a sharp enough eye, you can split each of the two loops for a total of four interlinked loops.

Now, for a real mind-boggler, make another loop with only half a twist, like the first one. This time, instead of cutting it down the middle, half-and-half, cut to one side, into sections one-third and two-thirds as wide as the original. You'll find you have to go around twice before your cut meets itself; and you'll also find, believe it or not, that what you get is two interlinked loops, one of them twice as long as the other.

You can try more twists and more styles of slicing the strip, getting something different every time. For instance, a strip with two full turns in it, cut down the middle, yields two loops linked in a kind of true-love-knot affair. The possibilities are endless. Of course, you might get still more attention if you pulled these stunts while driving a Porsche, but we can't tell you how to make one of those.

THE COFFEE-CAN
BOOMERANG

Even show-offs would live in a better world if there weren't so much junk lying around, right? People who litter the earth with old tin cans are not show-offs, just slobs.

When the show-off throws away a tin can, it doesn't just lie there. No sir! It comes right back! Then the show-off lovingly picks it up, dusts it off, and puts it on the shelf with the rest of his show-off equipment. Here's how to build the mysterious returning tin can and fascinate everybody on your block, especially the hound dogs.

Collect an ordinary coffee can (empty), two big matches (or sticks about the same size), an office rubber band, and a couple of lead wall anchor plugs from the hardware store (or big fishing sinkers, or anything that's small and heavy). Punch a hole right in the middle of each end of the coffee can—the fixed end, and the lid. See figure 1 for the correct arrangement.

If you're using lead anchor plugs, fasten them together with a hefty piece of tape (figure 2) and then tape them to the middle of the rubber band (figure 3). If you have a big

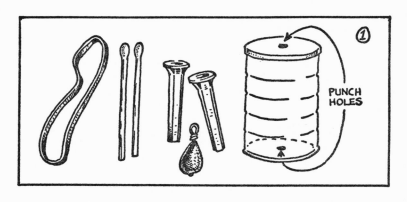

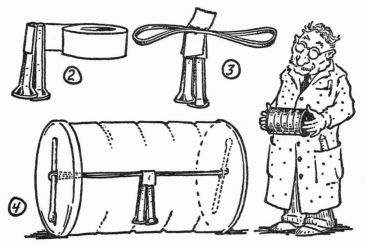

sinker, just put it in the middle of the rubber band with a knot.

Thread the rubber band through the holes in the ends of the can, and hold it there with the match sticks (figure 4). The rubber band should be tight enough to keep the weights from striking the sides of the can, when the can is in a horizontal position.

When everything is finished as in figure 4, just roll the can away from you. This will take a stronger and smoother push than you think. Now watch! As the can rolls away, the weights wind up the rubber band. The can stops. Then it rolls right back to you. Fantastic.

For a superior, more mysterious version of the coffee-can boomerang, you could conceal the presence of the rubber band by screwing two screw-eyes in two small blocks of wood, gluing the blocks to the inside of the can-lids with epoxy, and stringing the band between the hooks. But maybe you'd better not. If you show off too brilliantly, even the dogs will begin to resent you.

HOW TO UNCRUSH A
BEER CAN

Much have we travelled in the realms of gold, fellow show-offs, and we've revealed to you many a mystery, by all the odds the most useful was when we showed you how to crush a steel beer can in that wonderful, indispensable book *Sneaky Feats* (Sheed & Ward, 1975). Now, assuming you know how to crush a beer can, we're going to show you, for a change, something perfectly useless and, in its slow-moving way, equally spectacular: how to *uncrush* a beer can. For this purpose, we've adopted the method used by Francis Galton, author of the nineteenth-century classic *The Art of Travel*, for taking the dents out of canteens. Canteens are few and far between, these days, and they don't dent because they are made of plastic. But a classic is a classic, and this knowledge must not perish from the earth.

First, crush a beer can. This time, don't use one of the hard-to-find but totally superior steel kind; get the ordinary, new-fangled aluminum sort, because it works better. And don't crush it too much; enough will be enough. Just make your point; batter it up good but don't destroy it.

Take your crushed beer can and fill it up, through the hole, right to the brim with dried split peas—yellow or green makes no difference. When it won't hold any more, pour some water in until it won't hold any more water either. Put it in the sink, right side up. After about an hour, add some more water to replace any that's soaked into the peas.

Nothing will happen for what seems an eternity. Then, after two or three hours, the peas begin to swell up. With irresistible force, the peas will expand. With little shrieks and creaks, the knocks and dents in the beer can will be ironed out by expanding peas.

Finally, the swelling peas will restore the can to its original pristine condition. If this doesn't quite happen, shake and scrape out the peas and give it a refill and some more time.

Once you start the peas swelling, it is unnecessary, of course, to touch the can with the human hand again. This is the point at which to place your bets; the strongest person you know will be unable to do with both hands what you can do with none, if only you've got some peas and some patience.

THE EXPLORER'S NEEDLE

Suppose you're misplaced in Africa or some other confusing part of the earth, don't speak the local language, and wish to know which way is north. If that's too much supposing, just suppose you're messing around the house on a rainy day and want to exhibit your mastery of the principles of surface tension and magnetism to an admiring audience of one or more. Whichever you'd rather suppose, here's a snazzy way to suppose it, with the help of a few simple household articles.

For the first part of this stunt we thank Dave Black of Fort Wayne, Indiana, who points out that if you are very careful you can make a needle (or a straight pin) float in the surface tension on top of a glass of water. Since many straight pins are made of nonmagnetic brass, use a steel needle if you want to proceed to part two.

For part one, all you do is fill up a glass of water, let it settle quietly, and gently, gently, place a small steel needle flat on top of the water. Miraculous! It floats! If your hand isn't steady enough to make it float, do what Dave Black does: cut a square of tissue a little bigger than the

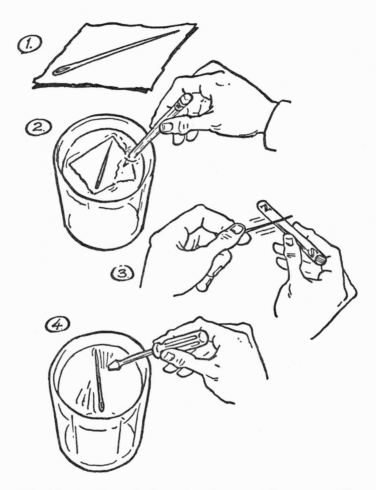

needle (figure 1) and place the tissue on the water. Then put the needle on the tissue and help the tissue to sink with gentle pokes of a pencil (figure 2), leaving the needle floating on the surface.

Once you've learned to float the needle, proceed to part two of the Explorer's Needle by picking up the needle, drying it off, and magnetizing it by stroking it a few times with a magnet (figure 3). A big powerful magnet is not necessary—the little round ones used to stick messages to the refrigerator will do the job, since the needle need not be very powerfully magnetized. After giving the needle a few strokes, float it again as you did before. Slowly, slowly, it will turn on the surface until it comes to rest pointing north and south, and presto, you've made a magnetic compass.

For a further exhibitionistic trick, you can use your magnetized floating needle to demonstrate that the world is full of magnets. Practically everything made of steel in the house is slightly magnetized, just as a result of being banged around in the earth's magnetic field. Under normal circumstances this magnetism is too weak to sense, but if you just reach into your tool drawer and pull out an old screwdriver, you'll probably find that while it attracts one end of your floating needle, it repels the other end (figure 4), thus illustrating what you learned in school about magnets. If this doesn't work with the screwdriver, try the pliers; and if nothing you can find seems to work quite right, at least you've got your compass and can locate your way out of Africa!

THE KWICK-'N-EEZY
FILET DE BOEUF WELLINGTON

Everybody envies a great cook, one of those people who can, at vast expense and with infinite skill and labor and careful attention to Escoffier, whip up a great classic specialty like Beef Wellington—that tender filet bathed in delicate mushrooms and the very best goose-liver paté, all wrapped up in flaky pastry and done to tender perfection. To be a great cook takes a lifetime of hard work—too hard for show-offs. Everybody will envy you almost as much if you can just fake it in about half an hour with easy every-day ingredients. Here's how to be envied almost as much as a great cook, and produce results nothing short of spectac-ular. So what if the Galloping Gourmet can do better?

Buy the tail end of a filet of beef—about a one-pound chunk. Cut the fat (figure 1) out of the middle, and soak the meat for a while in Lea & Perrins sauce, or a superior marinade of your own devising, if you insist. Tie it up with string, rolling into a shapely chunk (figure 2). Note that this is not rolled end-to-end like a jelly roll, just sideways until snug.

Put the beef in a pan and stick it in a very hot oven for

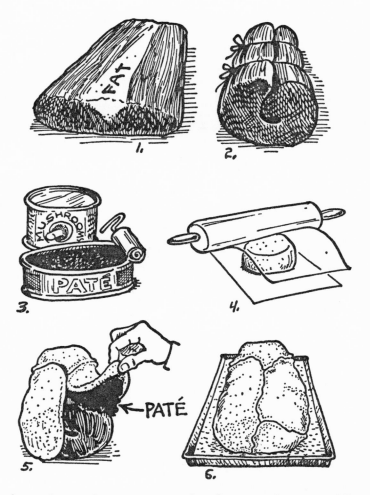

about four minutes, to set the shape of the meat. Meanwhile, take a four-ounce can of mushrooms (or fresh if you can get them), drain and blot dry with a towel, chop very fine, and mix them up with a four-ounce can of liver paté—the quality is up to you (figure 3).

Quick, now, open a can of refrigerator biscuits, put a biscuit between two sheets of waxed paper and roll it flat, into a long oval (figure 4), about as long as the meat. Spread the biscuit with some of the paté-mushroom goo, untie the meat, and put it on the paté-spread biscuit. Roll out more biscuits and wrap them around the meat, like tiles, first spreading the meat with the paté mixture (figure 5).

Notice how the meat has a sort of V-shaped slot on top? Fill the V with the mushroom goo, and keep tiling the meat with rolled biscuits. As you go, seal the edges of the biscuits by squeezing them gently together. It helps if you don't get the edges slippery with paté mixture. Milk can be used for glue to help hold the edges together.

When the whole filet is tiled up, cook at 450 degrees on a big flat pan until the outside is well browned. The meat will be rare and tender, and the whole thing will resemble one of those lumpy knotted breads you see in German bakeries (figure 6).

To serve, slice with a very sharp knife and just, well, serve. Go ahead and let everybody at dinner think it's just bread, until, with a flourish of your razor-keen carver, you reveal your tantalizing surprise and emit the show-off's war cry: "I bet you can't do this!"

ACKNOWLEDGMENTS

Sneaky Feats

For the following contributions sent by our far-flung friends and correspondents, the authors of this book are truly grateful—so grateful that we are putting their names right here, in actual print. Mothers of our correspondents, please join with us in recognition of your exhibitionist offspring.

Bob Brown (How to make custom-made money)
Mr. and Mrs. A. Delcorio (How to be calculating)
Priscilla Eakeley (How to be a twenty-card wizard)
J.O. Ferrell (How to be very, very incombustible)
Marjorie Kanehl (Two tricks for a buck)
Bette Palmer (Whistling through grass)
Dominic Valentine (Testing your strength)

We are also grateful to *Esquire's* contributing editor Philip Nobile, in real life an acquisitions editor for Sheed & Ward, who introduced us to his boss, after which things got moving real quick.

More Sneaky Feats

We would like to recognize the contributions of our friends, correspondents and relations toward making this book what it is today. Our thanks pour forth to the following exhibitionists, many of whom deserve better things than being put on a list like this. We hope they get them:

Dave Black (The Explorer's Needle)
Jeff Brown (Kiss a String and Make It Well)
Carmen Buccola (Look, Ma, One Hand)
Gil Eisner (Dinner Music for the Spoon Player)
Sarah Ferrell (How to Mug Yourself)
Ken Geisel (The Invaluable One-Dollar Ring)
Joseph C. Poley (Strung Up by the Buttonhole)
Bruno Profumo (Slipping the Cuffs)
James Weaver (Off to Phone the Wizard)
Otho C. Woods (The Five-Cent Solution)

Tom Ferrell and Lee Eisenberg, coauthors of the nationally syndicated column *The Show-Off*, are both residents of New York and editors at *Esquire* magazine.

Tom Ferrell, managing editor at *Esquire* magazine, graduated from Stanford University. He joined *Esquire* in 1966 as a Ph.D. dropout from Harvard. He was born in Joplin, Missouri.

Lee Eisenberg, senior editor at *Esquire,* was born in Philadelphia in 1946, received his B.A. and M.A. degrees from the University of Pennsylvania. He lectures at New York University. His work has appeared in *Rolling Stone,* the *New York Times Book Review* and *National Review.*